Let's Be Reasonable

Let's Be Reasonable

*A Conservative Case for
Liberal Education*

Jonathan Marks

PRINCETON UNIVERSITY PRESS
PRINCETON & OXFORD

Copyright © 2021 by Princeton University Press

Requests for permission to reproduce material from this work
should be sent to permissions@press.princeton.edu

Published by Princeton University Press
41 William Street, Princeton, New Jersey 08540
99 Banbury Road, Oxford OX2 6JX

press.princeton.edu

All Rights Reserved
First Paperback Printing, 2023
Paperback ISBN 9780691207728
Cloth ISBN 9780691193854
ISBN (e-book) 9780691207711
Library of Congress Control Number: 2020946849

British Library Cataloging-in-Publication Data is available

Editorial: Peter Dougherty and Alena Chekanov
Production Editorial: Karen Carter
Text and Jacket/Cover Design: Karl Spurzem
Production: Erin Suydam
Publicity: James Schneider and Kate Farquhar-Thomson
Copyeditor: Karen Verde

This book has been composed in Arno Pro with Bodoni Std and
Bauer Bodoni 1 display

For Anna

CONTENTS

PREFACE

There cannot be anything so disingenuous, so misbecoming a
gentleman or anyone who pretends to be a rational creature,
as not to yield to plain reason and the conviction of clear
arguments.

—JOHN LOCKE, *SOME THOUGHTS
CONCERNING EDUCATION*

The field of reason teems with people who are putting us on.
When we exclaim "be reasonable!" we're often addressing
someone who makes arguments but will never be convinced by
one, a bullshitter, or a shill, or our hyperpartisan social media
frenemy. What they lack in reason isn't a set of tools, packaged
by higher educators as "critical thinking," for their argument
building and repair projects. They can argue and evaluate arguments, sometimes with frustrating ingenuity and skill. What
they lack, whether because, like the bullshitter, they don't care
which argument is best, or because, like the hyperpartisan, they
care too much about the triumph of their team, is the disposition to treat reason not just as a tool but as an authority.

By "be reasonable!" we don't mean "mind your syllogisms!"
Behind our exclamation is a question: "Aren't you ashamed?"
Our way of talking captures the sense, still alive in us despite

the resolute unseriousness of public speech, that reason is not only an authority but also the kind of authority that is an honor to obey and a disgrace to betray, the sense that there's such a thing as conduct unbecoming a reasoner. The strength or weakness of that sense distinguishes competent users of reason, who may be highly skilled at making weak arguments seem strong, and reasonable people, between an intellectual community and a debate team. I was on the debate team, so I get the appeal. But the debater fears, as the political and educational philosopher John Locke puts it, "the disgrace of not being able to maintain whatever he has once affirmed"; he fears yielding to reason if that entails yielding to his opponent.[1] He doesn't fear the disgrace of clinging to an argument long after it has been refuted. This kind of clinging is the special province of pundits, spokespeople, and other hired guns, but we notice it, also, in our colleagues, classmates, neighbors and, if less often, ourselves.

This book makes a case for liberal education, whose aim is becoming reasonable in the sense outlined above, an aim demanding enough that falling short of it is the repeated experience not only of students but also of their teachers. We can't afford to be distracted from it, but we are. The distinction between reasonable people and skilled arguers, an echo of the ancient distinction between philosophers and sophists, is at best an intermittent concern even for colleges and universities that proudly display liberal education on their banners.

This book also makes a conservative case for liberal education. Get out your camera, for here is that rare beast, the conservative professor. I admit it, not only on the occasional anonymous survey but also in the pages of conservative outlets like *Commentary Magazine* and the late, lamented, *Weekly Standard*. These are my credentials. But I should also explain what kind of conservative I am and what that has to do with reason, if only to counter a stereotype we'll come across later. When professors are asked why conservatives are scarce in academia, many reply that conservatives are closed-minded, an explanation that is itself closed-minded.

The political philosopher Leo Strauss quipped that one "of the most conservative groups here calls itself Daughters of the American Revolution." The "conservatism of our age is identical with what originally was liberalism," according to which governments, instituted to secure rights, and limited in scope, derive their legitimacy from the consent of the governed.[2] Liberalism, so understood, has more than one parent, but the foremost is Locke. No less a conservative than George Will puts Locke at the heart of the American Founding, and conservatives "seek to conserve" not the throne or the altar but "the American Founding."[3] I'm with him. I won't blame everything I say about conservatism on George Will, but I do claim that my position, though less fashionable than it once was, is in the conservative mainstream.

Conservatives like me suppose that the capacity to reason well is widely distributed. Thomas Jefferson wrote that the Declaration of Independence articulated "the common sense of the subject" of American rights and British wrongs "in terms so plain and firm as to command . . . assent."[4] He anticipated that "the free right to the unbounded exercise of reason" would reinforce the principles of the Revolution and the prestige of governments devoted to them.[5] But—here's Will again—"the right to consent" affirmed in the Declaration "presupposes in the citizenry a certain threshold of rationality, hence a durable claim to respect."[6] This respect, as well as the need for a people to take the measure of governments acting in widely varied circumstances, requires "ongoing meditation on America's Founding" rather than rote recitation of its principles.[7]

Such meditation is a requirement of free government, but it's also, and not only in political matters, one of its finest fruits. "The right improvement and exercise of our reason," for Locke, is "the highest perfection that a man can attain to in this life."[8] It should be no surprise that conservatives who admire Locke also admire liberal education.

Yet our good cheer about liberalism is mixed with pessimism. That's partly because we have a dimmer view than progressives do of reason's power in politics. We're convinced, with Locke, whose *Of the Conduct of the Understanding* is a master class in the mind's failings, that it requires uncommon effort and vigilance to establish and maintain a zone of rationality in an area crowded with natural and artificial obstacles to reasoning. It is also because, though we favor liberalism, we think that all political orders have vices. With the political theorist Alexis de Tocqueville, we say that polities devoted to freedom and equality can make manifest the natural dignity, even greatness, of human beings. But we also say with Tocqueville that such polities can break the connections between person and person, present and past, so that "nothing is linked together."[9] Narrowed, isolated, and weakened, democratic citizens may be eager to give up on governing themselves intellectually and otherwise.

Finally, although we think that some arguments command assent, we're aware that knowledge is elusive. Even in the matters that concern us most, and even when we can calmly think things through, we may gain no more than modest confidence that we have hold of the truth. Reasonable people disagree, and so, like Locke, we conservatives value "the opposite arguings of men of parts, showing the different sides of things and their various aspects and probabilities."[10] We're partisans, yes, but not in the scorched-earth style.

This version of conservatism is friendlier than others to liberal education, but it's not the only version that has favored or should favor it. Since the middle of the twentieth century, American conservatism has been a "movement of ideas," whose intellectuals have tried not only to change the world but also to understand it and persuade others that their understanding is reasonable.[11] Conservatives have been spirited, usually confident, participants in the battle of ideas. Even when liberal education hasn't followed naturally from their principles, they've sometimes championed it as giving a hearing to conservative ideas that might otherwise be neglected. This stance has certainly included attacks, fair and unfair, on our colleges and universities, and on their use as a platform for left activism. But it hasn't been despairing, as the conservative view of universities now threatens to be.

If conservative arguments for liberal education can seldom be heard today over the denunciations, that may be because many conservatives have lost confidence in their prospects in the battle of ideas.

In his 2016 essay, "The Flight 93 Election," Michael Anton, one of few intellectuals to back Donald Trump before he was elected, derided those who still think such a battle worth fighting. Conservatives spend "several hundred million dollars a year on think-tanks, magazines, conferences, fellowships, and such, complaining about this, that, the other, and everything." Words, words, words, many of them spoken on the "fundraising circuit." Wake up. The battle of ideas is over. The left won. Consequently, we have a "tidal wave of dysfunction, immorality, and corruption." America is a "cancer patient." Sure, Anton admits, a Trump presidency may be disastrous, but if Clinton wins, "death is certain." The conservative scribblers and chatterers who reject Trump are part of an unholy alliance of "America's ruling and intellectual classes." They're motivated by "pay-checks" and the desire to be accepted.[12] When conservative intellectuals huff about being reasonable, they mean that they've got theirs and to hell with the country.

As for universities, they're "wholly corrupt" and at the service of the globalist, left-progressive, "junta," to whom they feed our young.[13] Universities say they're devoted to "the free search for truth and its free exposition."[14] But smart conservatives in the Anton mold know that universities lie. When professors huff about being reasonable, they mean, "Do what progressives say, not what your rube parents say." From the outside, then, conservatives rail against universities. Sometimes, there are forays in to deliver "Socialism Sucks" merchandise to besieged conservative students and to goad the natives into discrediting themselves. But it's naïve to take universities seriously when they pledge allegiance to reason, and today's conservatives, toughened by the blows of an unremittingly hostile left-wing order, are nothing if not hard-nosed.

Some left-wing academics, too, we'll see, argue that universities feign allegiance to reason while they groom students to serve corrupt masters. These masters—neoliberals, Zionists, white supremacists, and so forth—aren't the same junta that conservatives take to be in charge. But the upshot is the same. When universities invoke "the free search for truth and its free exposition," they mean, "Look over there while we take your money and rationalize oppression." The academic left, being on the inside, has some hope for universities. But its resistance from within includes resistance to the pretense that universities are anything other than political tools. Today, the bad guys control the universities. Come the revolution, the good guys will. But it's naïve to take universities seriously when they talk reason, and today's radicals, toughened by the blows of an unremittingly hostile right-wing order, are nothing if not hard-nosed.

Not only from the right, then, but also from the left, colleges and universities are accused of paying lip service to reason and real service to another, wicked, master. Who says bipartisanship is dead?

If the nightmare visions of higher education to which I've alluded are true to life, then one may as well not aspire to turn professors and students to the work of becoming reasonable people. But those visions aren't true to life. I won't stint on criticizing colleges and universities. But the charge that they prepare students for enslavement to a progressive or conservative oligarchy that has higher education under its thumb is inaccurate and unjust. Because I'm a conservative, persuading conservatives of this is a goal near to my heart. But I write for anyone looking for an alternative to the despair that passes for realism in our understanding of the present and possible future of college.

That alternative isn't dewy optimism. Becoming reasonable, my kind of conservative avers, is hard and always unfinished work. Still, in a different context—speaking of liberal democratic communities—my friend, the political theorist, Steven Kautz, said, "Perhaps our hopes from reason were too great, but that is surely not a sound basis for abandoning reason, or for repudiating the many victories of reason over the forces of prejudice."[15] That sounds right for academic communities, too. Universities that make "Become reasonable!" their motto will not easily live up to it and can't be certain that students, parents, legislators, and philanthropists will buy it. But this uncertainty isn't cause for despair.

I doubt that we who defend liberal education are going down, but there are worse things than to go down swinging.

ACKNOWLEDGMENTS

In more than thirty years at colleges and universities, I've racked up too many debts to name, much less repay. Let me name some.

To begin with those most recently accrued, I'm indebted to my dear friend and colleague, Paul Stern, who urged me to write this book, talked me through much of it, commented on every chapter, and held my nose to the grindstone at a crucial moment.

I'm indebted to Carlin Romano, who helped me get a start at writing about higher education, pushed me to adapt my style to a new audience, and answered every question I had about how to get a book published and read.

I'm indebted to Peter Dougherty, an editor who knows how to handle an anxious author and on whose advice I've relied. He found two insightful anonymous reviewers, who challenged me to improve my argument and its presentation.

I'm most indebted to my wife, Anna, and not only because she lent me her editorial judgment. Authors are in danger, on the one hand, of overestimating the importance of what they're doing and, on the other, of thinking that they should quit. Anna, as ever, mocked and encouraged as needed to keep things level. This book is dedicated to her. My sons, Samuel and Benjamin, joined in the mockery and occasionally allowed themselves to be questioned about the habits of the young.

For their help with a knotty chapter, I'm indebted to Win Guilmette and David Lay Williams. For his good counsel on tone, I'm
indebted to Leon Kass. For her willingness to field dumb questions about data, I'm indebted to Anne Karreth. For his constant encouragement of my work, I'm indebted to Bob Brown.

For the opportunity to present a chapter of this book at the
University of Houston, I'm indebted to Jeremy Bailey and the
Jack Miller Center for Teaching America's Founding Principles
and History.

For generous financial support in different stages of writing
the book, I'm indebted to the Institute for Humane Studies and
the Charles Koch Foundation.

Let me acknowledge, too, some older debts. At the University of Chicago, I was lucky to find teachers from whose example I benefited and still benefit immeasurably, including Allan
Bloom, Daniel Brudney, Joseph Cropsey, Christine Korsgaard,
Ralph Lerner, Nathan Tarcov, and Karl Weintraub. At Michigan
State University, as a teaching novice, I leaned on the wisdom
of Richard Zinman and the friendship of Ron Lee.

Finally, for many good conversations about our common
work, I'm indebted to colleagues and friends over years at Car-
thage College and Ursinus College, including Maria Carrig,
Ellen Dawley, Robert Dawley, Rebecca Evans, Stew Goetz,
Sheryl Goodman, Win Guilmette, Steve Hood, Bill Kuhn, Re-
becca Lyczak, Chris Lynch, Tony Nadler, Marla Polley, Nathan
Rein, Charles Rice, Christian Rice, Kelly Sorensen, Paul Stern,
Paul Ulrich, Jon Volkmer, and Rich Wallace.

Last, I'm indebted to my students, from those who watched
me struggle against a monotone in early days to those watching
me struggle to master remote learning best practices today.
Their willingness to meet their teachers at least halfway, even
now, speaks well of them. Without idealizing the classroom,
I've tried to do them justice.

Let's Be Reasonable

CHAPTER ONE

Holding Harvard to Its Word

Convictions

This book is animated by several convictions. Here's one story, straight out of Cambridge, to cover them all. Late in 2015, at Annenberg Dining Hall, hungry Harvard undergraduates got a prize with their meals: the Holiday Placemat for Social Justice.[1]

The Holiday Placemat for Social Justice instructed students headed home for the holidays on how best to pierce the resistant skulls of their unwoke relatives regarding various issues, including student activism, Islamophobia, and "Black Murders in the Street." The placemat also covered a Harvard-specific issue, namely the title, "Master." Harvard had dropped this title for dormitory heads because some students associated it with slavery, although, as no one disputes, Harvard's use of "Master" had nothing to do with slavery. The complaint, articulated by elite students, was no more defensible than the demand, made by the regular folk students at Lebanon Valley College, to change the name of Lynch Hall because it reminded them of lynching.[2] Nonetheless, Harvard's placemats urged students not to back down, no matter how much less awkward it might make Christmas dinner. They were to say, perhaps with a smirk, that "it doesn't seem onerous" to change the name. Uncle Trumpkin, one presumes, would be struck dumb.

This placemat had been distributed not by enterprising liberal students, but by administrators, the Freshman Dean's Office and the Office of Equity, Diversity, and Inclusion. When word got out, Harvard tried Harvard-splaining. Don't worry that we're mobilizing our students to proselytize for the left because, as one dean said, it's "not that you have to believe in what's on the placemat." No coercion, no foul.

Another dean suggested that the placemats would encourage dialogue, which might also have been said of placemats that endorsed Jill Stein or denounced sex out of wedlock. A schoolchild could see through this defense. Accordingly, eighteen members of Harvard's Undergraduate Council signed a letter reminding Harvard's leaders of what they should have known—prescribing "party-line talking points stands in stark contrast to the College's mission of fostering intellectual, social, and personal growth."[3] Perhaps administration officials looked it up in the catalog and realized that their undergraduates knew Harvard's mission better than they did. More likely, Harvard didn't want to dig itself a deeper publicity hole. The offices responsible for the placemats apologized.

What can we learn from this incident? First, it's interesting that we know about it. Okay, it's Harvard. But isn't it strange that dining hall news caught coverage from major outlets, from Fox News to CNN? Journalists love a "Look, the campus lefties are at it again!" story.

One conviction, then, that I have about higher education is that its story is poorly told. Larry Summers, former president of Harvard, admits to "a great deal of absurd political correctness" at universities. But, he says, "The main thing that's happening is what always happens: professors teach courses, students take courses, students aspire to graduate, they make friends, they plan their lives, they have a formative experience, they are educated." Anyone "who thinks that's not the main thing going on on college campuses is making a mistake."[4] As a freelance higher education writer, I regularly scan the academic ocean for the equivalent of shark attacks. But as a professor with more than two decades of experience, acquired at four different institutions of higher learning, I know that Summers is right. Most days, there are no shark attacks. But even in higher education news, if it bleeds it leads.

Although news about campus activists occasionally makes the *New York Times*, one more often sees campus shark attack stories in conservative outlets, since professors are among the elites whom conservative populists love to hate. American conservatives have been taking professors to task at least since William F. Buckley's *God and Man at Yale*. But that book could be characterized, in George Will's words, as a "lovers' quarrel."[5] Decades after *God and Man*, Buckley's *National Review* published an article by Allan Bloom, which grew into the bestselling *The Closing of the American Mind*, a book that, whatever fault it found in them, was full of love for universities. Bloom, the teacher who got me into this mess, was no conservative,[6] but the *National Review*'s association with him shows that it wasn't so long ago that conservatives thought universities were worth fighting for. Such conservatives still exist, but the dominant strain in contemporary conservatism is done with the lovers' quarrel, in the midst of a bitter divorce, and more inclined to murder its ex than to try to win her back.

Another conviction of mine is that conservatives shouldn't give up on universities.

Yet the Harvard placemat story backs up the academy's conservative critics. The left is so embedded not only at left-branded places like Oberlin and Berkeley but also at "grandees 'r' us" Harvard that one no longer needs student activists and radical professors with imposing beards to march around and demand things. After the shouts of activists subside, the news trucks depart; but the droning of deans, where the campus action is, continues. It's hard to know whether the activists of the sixties, who worried about being co-opted, would feel triumphant or dismayed at how college administrators have, without fanfare, taken up their cause. "Of course we're distributing social justice placemats," they seem to tell us; "Why all the fuss?"

Another conviction that led me to write this book, then, is that colleges and universities harm their reputations and missions by adopting, even in this snoozy way, the language and priorities of one branch of the left. I doubt I'll persuade many campus activists, who seem almost as hot to tear the university down as their conservative adversaries. But I hope to lure from the sidelines some of the many professors, administrators, alumni, and students who dislike controversy. The left has more power on campus than it has numbers because other stakeholders, as they say in the movies, don't want no trouble.

One other observation about the curious case of Harvard's holiday placemat: contrary to the widespread view that students, especially elite students, are coddled whiners, some of Harvard's students are the heroes and heroines of the tale. Members of the Undergraduate Council, whether they agreed or disagreed with the points the placemats promulgated, didn't want to be spoon-fed. They rebelled against their keepers for "telling them what to think and what to say."[7] They demanded to be treated as reasonable people.

College students aren't, as some on the left would have it, moral exemplars at whose feet their degreed but clueless caretakers, born prior to the discovery of justice, could profitably sit. But they also aren't, as some on the right would have it, cry-bullies who should be given a stern lecture about real hardship before we expel them without their suppers. Whatever closed-mindedness students exhibit isn't obviously worse than that of their elders. Whatever suspicion students have of the glories of speech and debate is partly justified by the stupidity and insincerity of what passes for public discussion. Without romanticizing college students, we should be able to imagine that a non-trivial number of them will respond to an education that makes free discussion seem at all attractive.

That brings me to a final conviction. Colleges and universities should respond to and cultivate in students that in them which responds to the summons, "Become reasonable!" Locke, the philosopher of freedom, was also a philosopher of discipline. In *Some Thoughts Concerning Education*, he aims at the cultivation of "right reasoning [in order] to have right notions and a right judgment of things, to distinguish between truth and falsehood, right and wrong, and to act accordingly." The products of Lockean education will feel and think that there can be nothing so "misbecoming a gentleman, or anyone who pretends to be a rational creature, as not to yield to plain reason and the conviction of clear arguments."[8] The discipline of yielding to and acting on reasonable arguments, rather than impulses, tribal loyalties, or superstitions, protects one's freedom and can be a source of pride. There's something appealing about education in such a discipline.

I don't claim that liberal education properly understood greatly resembles the education of Locke's *Thoughts*, much of which is about pre-adolescents. Nor do I claim that the intellectual freedom experienced by Lockean citizens is the peak of intellectual freedom. Socrates, the patron saint of liberal educators, about whom we'll hear more later, arguably guides us to still greater peaks. What I'll claim is that even those who can imagine higher heights would raise a glass if we had in our colleges and universities communities of students and faculty who considered it a disgrace not to listen to reason. We'd raise several more if our students carried that standard of praise and blame into their lives after college. Universities, as if bored with what they call "critical thinking," have unfurled a multitude of other banners sporting other terms: diversity, empathy, world citizenship, civic engagement, and so on. But the work of cultivating the reason, and pride in being reasonable, of which Locke writes, is difficult. If universities, distracted by other things, fail at it, students and graduates marching under those other banners are unlikely to do themselves or others much good.

I aim especially to defend that last conviction. Colleges and universities will do better at justifying themselves, at guarding students against foolishness and fanaticism, and at preparing them to exercise good judgment, if they focus more single-mindedly on shaping students in the mold of the person Locke describes. We're no gentlemen, Lockean or otherwise. But we profess ourselves rational creatures. Our colleges and universities need to do everything they can to ensure that we're not mere pretenders when we claim to found our judgments about true and false, good and bad, right and wrong, on more than passion or prejudice. That's a worthy aim for liberal education.

A Failure and a Success at Explaining Liberal Education

Early in my career, on my way to a job interview, I was forced to talk to a man jammed next to me on the airplane. Like many professors, I shouldn't be allowed out in public, but at least I know it. So I had gone to great lengths to avoid conversation.

I buried my face in a book; I played dead. But my neighbor was persistent and got me to talk about my work.

Remember: I was on my way to an interview. Thus prepared, I told him that I'm a teacher and that I bring my students into close contact with great thinkers who challenge their prejudices, goad them to think for themselves, and exemplify how to think well about important and elusive things. I told him that I'm also a scholar, engaged in the same work I ask my students to do. At the time, I was writing an essay on the eighteenth-century political philosopher, Jean-Jacques Rousseau. Reading Rousseau, I explained, clarifies, and suggests serious objections to, the way in which certain politicians and philosophers have tried to found politics on compassion. This was, I must say, my best stuff.

After a long pause, my new acquaintance said, "I wish I could say that sounded interesting."

Fast forward to 2013. I'd written an op-ed for the *Wall Street Journal* about the anti-Israel movement in academia, about which I'll say more in chapter 5. Bob, an alumnus of Ursinus College, where I teach, wrote to me. My argument, he said, confirmed his opinion that a too-liberal academia was ruining young minds. Thanks to me, he felt great about his decision, made years earlier, to stop giving money to Ursinus.

Sorry bosses.

I responded to Bob's letter, making a pitch for Ursinus not unlike the one I'd made for myself on the airplane, refined, I hope, over the decades. We struck up a friendship. Bob is a retired doctor who served in the US Navy, just missing action in World War II, and who re-enlisted for Vietnam. After the war, he spent many unpaid hours helping people who needed medical care, near home and abroad. If Bob, who had risked his own life, saved the lives of others, and delivered many, many babies, had said his life was more admirable than mine, I wouldn't have contradicted him.

Yet Bob, a self-described conservative, respected professors. At Ursinus, he'd focused on preparing for medical school and, since he had to work to afford his education, had time for little else. Later on, however, Bob sought out some of the same minds that I introduce my students to, including Socrates's student, Plato. He had struggled with Plato. Who doesn't? Thomas Jefferson once complained of Plato's "sophisms, futilities, and incomprehensibilities."[9] But Bob was more than ready to believe that he'd missed something worth knowing. He thought and thinks that a person who can help him understand philosophers like Plato, and so help him make better sense of things, deserves high respect.

Perhaps Bob has more respect for professors than our capacity to educate warrants. But from my friendship with him, I draw two conclusions. First, even those most angered at the stories they read about universities may not be badly disposed toward them or the work that most professors and students do. It would be comforting, in a way, if contempt for higher education were contempt for the life of the mind. If our accusers were proud ignoramuses, sure, we might all go down with the ship, but we could at least go down with smug expressions on our faces. No doubt some haters hate even our best work. But I doubt that Bob is the only lover of learning who disapproves of colleges because we've failed to make the best case for them. Which brings me to the second conclusion: Such a case might change minds. It's not comforting to think that we bear some of the blame for our own woes. Still less comforting is the possibility that we're not only bad at communicating our case to others but also not confident in it ourselves.

We Can Do Better Than This

Allan Bloom, in *The Closing of the American Mind*, wrote that professors of the humanities, tasked with "interpreting and transmitting old books," don't "believe in themselves or what they do." On the one hand, they're "old maid librarians" who don't imagine that the books they shyly love can be loved by the young. On the other hand, when they've tried to win the hearts of students, they've followed the un-shy example of 1960s professors, who looked for ways to incorporate "these tired old books" into "revolutionary consciousness."[10] This trend hasn't diminished since *Closing* came out in 1987 and helps explain why the Modern Language Association, officially dedicated to the study of language and literature, makes news mainly when its members debate the Israeli-Palestinian conflict. I will, as is practically required in a book of this kind, bemoan the influence of the academic left later. But despite the persistent misunderstanding of *Closing* as blaming all of the academy's troubles on leftists drunk on French theory, let's not forget those old maid librarians. They tell us that humanists wouldn't have gone in for politics if they'd thought they had something else of great worth to offer.

A similar diffidence weakens the case for liberal education. Many four-year colleges and universities invoke liberal education to signal that they offer more than specialized knowledge, job skills, and artisanal food. Yet when one orders a meaty explanation of liberal education, one is usually served word salad.

Sometimes, the salad is assembled by well-meaning and experienced teachers and scholars who have logged hours in lonely conference centers, thinking and talking about liberal education. Consider the Association of American Colleges and Universities (AAC&U), "the leading national association concerned with the quality, vitality, and public standing of undergraduate liberal education."[11] They meet regularly to discuss liberal education, have a journal called *Liberal Education*, and frequently communicate with the public about liberal education.

Here's the definition of "Twenty-First Century Liberal Education" that this reflection, discussion, and experience have produced.

> Liberal education is an approach to learning that empowers individuals and prepares them to deal with complexity, diversity, and change. It provides students with broad knowledge of the wider world (e.g. science, culture, and society) as well as in-depth study in a specific area of interest. A liberal education helps students develop a sense of social responsibility, as well as strong and transferable intellectual and practical skills such as communication, analytical and problem-solving skills, and a demonstrated ability to apply knowledge and skills in real-world settings.[12]

Inspired yet? If not, hear out Katherine Bergeron, president of Connecticut College, who, in an interview, pats her college on the back for, as the headline puts it, "Remaking the Liberal Arts."[13] This great remaking, like the AAC&U statement, assumes that the fresh new case for liberal education, the one that will grab the kids, their parents, and, let us pray, philanthropists, is that liberal education will henceforth help us deal with complicated things. With regard to its core requirements, Connecticut College's faculty "asked the question, does this make sense for . . . a global and networked twenty-first century?" No, they concluded, it didn't make sense because, although we've been talking about an increasingly interconnected world since the eighteenth century, prior curriculum architects were unaware that things are complicated.

And so, Connecticut College professors said stiltedly to themselves, we "need to create some new structures that help students deal with complexity because the goal of an education is to prepare students to confront the increasingly complex world problems." The main innovation of the new curriculum is the "integrative pathway," made up of a group of courses, in various disciplines, linked by a theme, through which students pursue a question they've chosen. This way of organizing part of a student's career builds on sensible propositions. Questions often have to be pursued across different areas of study, students are more likely to understand the importance of different modes of inquiry if they use them to pursue a question that interests them, and students should take some responsibility for shaping their own educations. That's good. But it's hard to see what the new curriculum aims at, apart from a graduate who is capable of dealing with complicated things and who's nice rather than naughty, for Connecticut College also embraces the AAC&U's goal of "social responsibility."

I don't mean to pick on Connecticut College, whose core looks better than most to me, or the AAC&U in particular, though campaigners for liberal education ought to be less diffuse and more inspiring. Unfortunately, from Harvard on down, the statements of purpose and principle that supposedly animate our colleges and universities may as well have been produced by Mad Libs. Adjectives, like integrative, interdisciplinary, interconnected, entrepreneurial, twenty-first century, complex, dynamic, and problem-solving, are distributed among brochures as if at random to make it appear that something buzzy is going on. In generating such language, we're not putting lipstick on a pig; there are many wonderful things going on at our colleges and universities. Rather, we're covering up our inability to state what the main aim of liberal education is by promising to tend to all aims and to be up to date, not to say cool.

Why This Book?

Liberal education is often explained poorly. But I've named one book that explains it well, *The Closing of the American Mind*. Allan Bloom wrote it more than thirty years ago.

From *Closing*, we learn that liberal education responds to the question "every young person asks: 'Who am I?'" which means, "'What is man?'" Teachers assist students in fulfilling "human nature against all the deforming forces of convention and prejudice." But in "our chronic lack of certainty" about how to answer the question of what we are and what the best way of life is, liberal education "comes down to knowing the alternative answers," many of which are to be found in books, "and thinking about them." The "liberally educated person" is free enough of the prejudices of her time and place to "resist the easy and preferred answers" to these questions.[14] Liberally educated people will almost certainly be good at dealing with complicated things, and may even be nice. But they'll also know what it's like to put the questions of what one is and of how one should live at the center of their concerns, and be familiar with the pleasure, usefulness, and freedom of conversing about those questions.

I think that liberal education so conceived can shape reasonable people, the shaping of whom I've proposed as liberal education's aim. I agree with Bloom, as I'll explain in chapter 3, that liberal education entails, though it's not exhausted by, attention to old books. Among the vices Tocqueville finds in modern democracy is that it fosters an "instinctive distaste for what is old."[15] This prejudice, "the belief," as Bloom puts it, "that the here and now is all there is," protects every other prejudice of our time by discrediting in advance appeals to the wisdom of other times.[16] This presentism isn't the only impediment to becoming reasonable, but it is among the most formidable. As the examples I use will make clear, I've been influenced by Bloom's charge to teach and learn from old books. *Closing* is still in print. So why make a case, again, for liberal education?

First, my book is concerned with the case for liberal education in this urgent moment. To be sure, when you read of, or, in my case, live in the midst of, debates over whether there are enough women or people of color in the curriculum, you might think you've stepped out of a time machine and into the early 1990s. But the challenges of one time are never quite the same as the challenges of another. The here and now isn't all there is, but sensible people attend to it.

In my career, I haven't witnessed as much anxiety about the future of colleges and universities as I see now. The first essay I wrote about higher education concerned the Massive Open Online Courses—MOOCs is their delightful acronym—that some commentators thought would upend, or just end, traditional higher education. If the most distinguished and charismatic professors could lecture to hundreds of thousands of students, each taking in the lecture and doing coursework on his or her own time, and the cost of that experience could be reduced to a tiny fraction of the cost of a class on a residential campus, many students, the argument went, would abandon brick-and-mortar colleges. Disruption was the word of the day.[17] Sebastian Thrun of Google and self-driving car fame had founded Udacity and was racing to offer college credits on the cheap. Thrun had predicted that there would be, in fifty years, only ten colleges and universities left in the world. My colleagues and I sat nervously in our offices, listing other jobs for which we were qualified. My list was short.

I thought then and think now that professors—we are as fretful as we are socially inept—were overreacting to MOOCs. It hardly seemed likely that saying "Look, now it's on a screen!" would cause many students to get better at absorbing lectures and educating themselves than they've proven to be historically. And Thrun was singing a different song the following year: "We don't educate people as others wished, or as I wished. We have a lousy product."[18]

Still, there's more pressure to explain the value of liberal education now than there has been. People for whom the long recession was a fresh memory even before the pandemic struck want, understandably, to be shown the money.

But there's also more opportunity to make a case for liberal education. Colleges and universities are desperately seeking to distinguish themselves.

I don't mean, although I wish to save my job as much as anyone, an opportunity to better the market position of liberal arts colleges like mine. No moral law requires my continued employment. Cathy Davidson, of the City University of New York, has the right idea when she says, "If we profs can be replaced by a computer screen, we should be."[19] The bosses will have to pry me out of my office with a crowbar, but they'll be right to do so if no good case can be made for choosing the kind of education I practice over cheaper varieties.

But I'm convinced that the guidance required to cultivate the kind of human being I've described with Locke's help doesn't scale. However good some televangelists may be at reaching into the souls of people they'll never meet, it's hard to see how reason and attachment to reason can be cultivated in students

by professors who know nothing about those students' prejudices, and the fears and hopes behind them. Our best hope for
success in that endeavor is to create a community, an intellectual community, in which our standards of praise and blame
suit people who seek the truth together.

I pause to acknowledge that this vision will have to contend
with actual student communities, in which the weekend sometimes starts on Thursday afternoon. Despite our best efforts to
bring the life of the mind into the dormitories, other concerns,
with drink, sex, sports, roommates, and creative combinations
thereof, often drown us out. Our goal isn't to make every college evening a night at the opera or every student into a pipe-
wielding, monocle-wearing intellectual. It is rather to cultivate
in our students an experience of and a taste for reflecting on
fundamental questions, for following arguments where they
lead, and for shaping their thoughts and actions in accordance
with what they can learn from those activities.

Here is a second reason for returning to the theme of liberal
education. Bloom reflected on "the kind of young persons who
populate the twenty or thirty best universities," like those he
taught at the University of Chicago.[20] That's not my sample. I've
spent the bulk of my career at Ursinus College and Carthage
College. Ursinus is, as I write, ranked eighty-two by *U.S. News*
among national liberal arts colleges. Carthage, to *U.S. News*, is
a regional rather than national college. Both provide superb
educations but either might be, as Ursinus is, listed among
"A+ schools for B students."

Most popular books on higher education are about super-
elite students. Think of William Deresiewicz's *Excellent Sheep*,
which is about how rough things are at Yale. Or they've been
written by professors or leaders at super-elite colleges. Think
of Andrew Delbanco's *College: What It Was, Is, and Should Be*

(Columbia), Michael Roth's *Beyond the University* (Wesleyan), and Anthony Kronman's *Education's End* (Yale, again).[21] I think Bloom was right that graduates of the top schools have "the greatest moral and intellectual effect on the nation." They demand our attention. But his book, a "report from the front" defined by our super-elite colleges, left room for a report from a different front, one occupied by students who haven't always been deemed suitable for liberal education. Perhaps they "lack the freedom to pursue a liberal education." Perhaps they "have their own needs and . . . very different characters from those" Bloom writes about.[22]

But perhaps they're not so different. I teach an essay by Earl Shorris, a public intellectual best known today for his work in education. The article isn't about my students, who on average are securely in the middle class, but about poor students who, at first glance, seem to lack the freedom to escape their neighborhoods, much less pursue a liberal education. Shorris did something that seemed crazy to me. Persuaded that the humanities, not job training, were the road out of poverty, he assembled a class consisting almost wholly of students at or below 150% of the poverty threshold. The class included homeless people. It included people who had been in prison and people who could barely read a tabloid newspaper. To this unlikely audience, Shorris proposed an education, which came to be called the Clemente Course, in philosophy, poetry, American history, logic, and art history.

Shorris told potential students that they would "have to read and think about the same kinds of ideas [they] would encounter in a first-year course at Harvard or Yale or Oxford." He told them, "You'll have to come to class in the snow and the rain and the cold and the dark. No one will coddle you, no one will slow down for you." There would be tests and papers and, upon successful completion, only a certificate, which Shorris couldn't promise would be accepted anywhere for college credit. He told them that if they were to take the class, it would have to be "because you want to study the humanities, because you want a certain kind of life, a richness of mind and spirit." One might think this pitch would empty a room of people barely getting by, but of "about twenty students" to whom Shorris first made it, "all but one . . . applied for admission."[23]

As I said, Shorris's idea sounded crazy to me, and even the frighteningly optimistic Shorris worried, especially about his neediest students. Why should people struggling through the month "care about fourteenth-century Italian painting or truth tables or the death of Socrates?"[24] In fact, nearly half failed to complete the course. But fourteen earned credit from Bard College, which had signed on, and Shorris's students proved to be interested in fourteenth-century Italian painting, truth tables, and the death of Socrates. To take one of many examples, here's Shorris on what happened after students were presented with a complex logic problem:

> When Sylvia and I left the Clemente Center that night, a knot of students was gathered outside, huddled against the wind. Snow had begun to fall, a slippery powder on the gray ice that covered all but a narrow space down the center of the sidewalk. Samantha and David stood in the middle of the group, still arguing over the answer to the problem.[25]

Here we have a small, engaged, community adjudicating a dispute about the truth by weighing the arguments.

Versions of the Clemente Course have since been offered to many students in many places, including to "internally displaced persons" from Darfur, in western Sudan, the site of a conflict that has caused unspeakable misery. Ismat Mahmoud

Ahmed, who helped teach the course, looks back on it: "At the beginning of the class, there was a prevailing feeling of despair, but as the study progressed that feeling was replaced by hope [;] this might be one of the reasons that strengthened my trust in philosophy."[26] This trust, as Shorris understands it, isn't that there is a straight road from liberal education to the alleviation of suffering. It's that even people in dire need and difficult circumstances can benefit from and experience happiness in the pursuit of what the social theorist W.E.B. Du Bois called the "riddle of existence." That riddle was once taught "in the groves by Plato" to aristocrats. In Du Bois's teaching days, at Atlanta University, it was taught to the children of freed slaves.[27]

Here, as a final witness, is a Clemente Course student, who had "escaped from a polygamous cult" some years prior to finding the course: "I was born with a giant question mark in my head." She had been taught that her inquisitiveness meant that there was something wrong with her. "I know," she said after experiencing the course, "that all the questions inside of me are freedom."[28]

Most of my students, again, are in the middle class. It's not absurd to think that this class is uncommonly cold to liberal education. On average, its members are comfortable enough not to yearn for liberation, but not so comfortable that they can easily be diverted from the question of how to make a living to the question of how one should live. Yet it is absurd to wring one's hands, as my colleagues and I sometimes do, and wonder if we dare present our students with an old book that speaks to enduring questions, rather than a new one that speaks to the questions of the moment. I've rarely known students to think any better about the latter sort of book, though professors and students alike may find the sailing smoother. It's not too much to expect that our students will prove as capable of entering into a conversation with Plato or Lincoln, or as open to being governed by the stronger argument, as Shorris's were.

I propose that the health of our civilization depends in part on meeting this expectation. I suspect that I've already taught more schoolteachers than many Harvard, Yale, and Princeton professors teach in an entire career. Graduates of our super-elite colleges don't pursue a teaching career in great numbers, except at the university level. Yet our future teachers should have at least as rich an education as our investment bankers and management consultants do. Du Bois, speaking of a group in direr straits than the American middle class, said that the most important purpose of "higher training schools" was "to furnish the black world with adequate standards of human culture and lofty ideals of life." Such schools would have to be staffed by "teachers of teachers" who would "so far as possible, be broad-minded, cultured men and women." They would practice an education that, though useful for breadwinning, "seeks as an end culture and character rather than breadwinning."[29]

Can any serious person claim that the teachers of our children shouldn't be broad-minded and cultured?

A Cautiously Optimistic Personal Note

I haven't always been optimistic about the prospects for liberal education outside of the top twenty or thirty schools. Like most people who pursue graduate training at those schools, I assumed—because attending top schools doesn't inoculate one from stupidity—that I'd teach at the kind of school I'd attended. But my first tenure track job was at Carthage College, of which almost no one I knew had heard. Not long before I started at Carthage, I heard an anxiety-provoking story from an acquaintance who had taught there, who was a dynamic, even fiery, lecturer. During one class, as he channeled the spirit of which-ever thinker was on the agenda, as he paced, gestured, and de-claimed, a student raised his hand. Did he have a question?

"Dude," the student drawled, "I don't know what you're talk-ing about."

Having come from the practically medieval University of Chicago, where professors were considered demigods, and where students were often turned on by old books, I wasn't sure I was ready to teach at Carthage. I worried that Greg Campbell, then president of the college, had overestimated our chances of launching, as he planned, a successful great books major there. But he was the boss, and they paid green dollars, so I did my part to develop the program.

My skepticism increased when my friend, Chris, suggested that a two-course sequence required for the new major, Foun-dations of Western Thought, should be taught in the style of seminars he had taken at his alma mater, St. John's College. In such team-taught seminars, one of the "tutors" poses a question meant to initiate a conversation about the book under consid-eration. Although tutors step in from time to time to participate in or guide the conversation, the seminar puts more responsi-bility on students to reason together about difficult questions than occurs in any other kind of class I've taught. St. John's stu-dents, though, are the kinds of weirdos who choose to attend a school built entirely around a great books curriculum. How would our Carthage students, who had made no such choice, fare with questions like these, which we confronted in different class sessions: (1) Why, according to Martin Luther, must we live on faith alone? How can one live on faith alone? (2) In *Anna Karenina* (our students read this vast Tolstoy novel in its entirety), Stiva and Levin exemplify different understandings of happiness and different understandings of love. Who is the superior man and who has the superior understanding? (3) What is nobility, according to Friedrich Nietzsche? What characteristics do noble people have? If Nietzsche is a fan of nobility, why does so much of what he says seem to undermine it?

Each of these questions included prefaces that helped our students to see why it might occur to thoughtful readers and to notice parts of our reading that could help. But our students didn't have the questions or any of the prefatory material before class began; having been asked only to read carefully, they were presented with the opening question in class. Thereafter, they were on their own for much of the session. We all, students and teachers, got used to, and began to take pride in, what teachers and students often find humiliating, namely, long silences. Several minutes would almost always pass before the first student, having gathered her thoughts enough to begin the conversation, spoke. But I was surprised, repeatedly, at the extent to which our refusal to seize the wheel was rewarded by our students. They'd uncover the same quotation or observation we might have brought in to advance the discussion, or find their footing in some other, unanticipated, way. I doubt that those students retained less than they would have had I lectured for the entire hour and forty-minute class period. I'm confident that many of them retained the experience of exploring, with the aid of the books and their peers, difficult questions whose bearing on their lives they could grasp.

At Ursinus College, I was lucky to work with President John Strassburger. Strassburger loved Abraham Lincoln and, like many such enthusiasts, had a high estimate of the possibilities of democracy and of democratic peoples. My experience at Carthage notwithstanding, I was skeptical of Strassburger's faith that our students, coming in with mostly modest high school accomplishments, could be made to embrace a required two-semester program, the Common Intellectual Experience, already in place when I got there. My Carthage students had at least elected to take a great books course. Every Ursinus first-year had to take the Common Intellectual Experience. All would be asked to pursue, with the help of texts like Plato's *Euthyphro* and Descartes's *Discourse on Method*, the questions around which the course revolved: How should one live? What does it mean to be human? What is the universe and what is my place in it? I was interested in those questions when I entered college, but I was, like those St. John's students, a bit of a weirdo.

As with most anything required, not every student embraces the Common Intellectual Experience. If you serve ice cream in a required course, there will be those who step forward to declare the flavors ill-chosen and the temperature intolerably cold. There are days when I wonder if it would be wiser to teach Rock Divas and their Discontents, which my students might find amusing, rather than the Book of Job, which my students find less "relatable." Yet on the days when the course works, and there are such days, my students seem to have the experience, which many of them recall as alumni, of becoming absorbed in and taking responsibility for a conversation that is no longer about school, or jumping through hoops for a good grade. The conversation is instead about how their convictions, of which they may have been only half-aware before they were asked to explain them, measure up under scrutiny and against competing convictions.

I now think that Presidents Campbell and Strassburger grasped something I didn't. I don't think that everyone should go to college, or that all students are capable of the same degree of intellectual independence, or that the quality of academic work on average can be the same at a Carthage or an Ursinus as it is at a Princeton. But I'm convinced by my experience in the programs those presidents championed that the capacity to benefit from a liberal education, and to become the kind of human being who takes pleasure and pride in trying to distinguish the true from the false, is widely distributed—a thought, as I noted in the preface, that informs the kind of conservatism I favor.

That thought is one plausible inference from an observation made by Tocqueville, who visited the United States in 1831–1832 and went on to write the most insightful work on democracy I know, *Democracy in America*. Tocqueville, who fears that democracy will snuff out greatness, nonetheless argues that it can make manifest "the natural greatness of man." Only in democracies does humanity itself, "man, taken apart from his time and his country and placed before nature and God with his passions, his doubts, his unheard of prosperity, and his incomprehensible miseries," become a fit object of poetry.[30]

Not that Tocqueville argued that universities should take the human situation he describes as its object. He thought that, at least in the nineteenth century, "the education of the greatest number" would have to be "scientific, commercial and industrial." The study of Greek and Latin literature might cause its practitioners, spoiled for moneymaking, to "trouble the state in the name of the Greeks and Romans instead of making it fruitful by their industry."[31] But we can only chuckle at the danger that our political world will be unsettled by pissed-off classicists. We are free to conclude that liberal education is one of few ways democracies have of raising up a present-minded, materialistic people to a kind of greatness.

This idea, democratic even in its recognition of democratic vices, helps explain why Locke inspires my argument. Locke's *Thoughts* concentrates on the education of gentlemen, who have the leisure to study and who, as members of England's governing class, will determine England's course and set its tone. It is not only a gentleman, however, but also "anyone who pretends to be a rational creature" who should learn to yield to "plain reason and the conviction of clear arguments." And, as Locke says in *Of the Conduct of the Understanding*, "Every man carries about him a touchstone, if he will make use of it, to distinguish . . . truth from appearances." That touchstone is "natural reason," a "noble faculty" possessed by "men of study and thought" and by "the day laborer," the differences between whom have more to do with experience and education than with inborn talent. Not everyone can be Einstein. But anyone can learn to "make use of better and surer principles" in deciding what to think about and how to act in matters that greatly concern them.[32] This is one way of understanding the natural greatness of man.

Perhaps, as two of Locke's most able interpreters observe, we can't help but ask whether Locke is too optimistic about the power of reason in human affairs.[33] Optimism about the capacity of students to be reasonable, for which I see some grounds in my teaching career, can't be a dogma for educators. But it seems the right starting point for liberal educators within democratic polities, which depend on the capacity of their citizens to be reasonable.

What's Not Coming and What Is

Two disclaimers. First, yes, I know. The higher education sector is vast and varied. We award more bachelor's degrees in parks, recreation, leisure, and fitness studies than we award in English. The eighteen- to twenty-one-year-old students I work with are different from the many older students attending college. Some students are homeless. Some struggle to afford nutritious food.

I wouldn't have brought up Earl Shorris and the Clemente Course if I thought that my argument mattered only to affluent eighteen- to twenty-one-year-olds. But as a preemptive attempt to fend off commentators who take any intervention in the higher education debate as an insult to their work, I acknowledge that my book won't solve all of higher education's problems. It won't house the homeless, feed the hungry, forgive student loans, or prevent the spread of mumps in the dorms. There's plenty of work to go around.

Second, and here I address my political philosophy friends, this isn't a work of high theory. I understand that in lumping together Du Bois, Locke, Socrates, and others, I'm neglecting important distinctions. There is a height at which the merit of an education that produces a Benjamin Franklin should be compared to an education that produces a Plato. But we're so far from that height that what those educations might have in common is more important for our purposes than what they might not. If my colleagues and I could shape a few Franklins, we wouldn't beat our breasts over not having shaped a Plato. We're modest that way.[34]

In this chapter, I've explained why I think my book is needed. Skepticism about, and even hostility toward, our colleges and universities may not be as deep as educators fear, but the bland and scattered justifications even liberal arts colleges offer for themselves do us no favors. And I've introduced becoming reasonable people as a worthy and inspiring aim for liberal education.

In the next, second, chapter, I clear some more ground for myself by addressing friends and critics of higher education on the left and the right. My fellow conservatives are right about the outsized influence of the left at many colleges and universities. Those who sympathize with the idea that universities are schools of reason should know how the embrace of left politics, though often half-hearted and bureaucratic, undermines that idea. But many conservatives overestimate the extent and depth of the problem and consequently consider universities lost. That hasn't always been the case for conservatives and shouldn't be the case now.

But enough ground-clearing. In the third chapter, I develop the idea of liberal education as the shaping of reasonable people and investigate its relationship to leading alternative ideas, that liberal educators should teach students to deal well with complexity and that liberal educators should shape students for citizenship. And I defend the aim of becoming reasonable as desirable, possible, and consistent with the aims of nearly all conservatives.

Here, though I know dissent is possible, I assume agreement that when we think, as in physics, about relations of cause and effect, we have reliable ways to distinguish between strong and weak arguments. Together, they constitute what we call scientific reason. Relations of cause and effect aren't limited to particles, and so this kind of reason has proven useful in my own field of political science in assessing, for example, whether a given policy has produced its desired outcome. But politics, and not only politics, turns in part on questions with which scientific reason doesn't much help, questions that present themselves to free persons trying to understand themselves, to make sense of their relations with others, and to form judgments where much is necessarily unknown to them. This abstract idea finds concrete expression in doubt, on the part of students and others, that there can be a rational approach to such questions. I follow others in arguing that there is such an approach, even if it doesn't offer the laws and formulas that scientific reason sometimes provides, and in naming this aspect of reason "judgment."

Long experience in the classroom gives me sympathy with the cry: "Great plan! Wake my students up when it's over!" In the fourth chapter, I consider students, what they are like—though I think they are much harder to know than one might imagine—and what they need from our colleges and universities. There are grounds for optimism about students, whom we're too apt to patronize or denounce.

Here I also take up the vexed issue of free speech on campus. We've been asking students to love a Wild West of speech in which they'll derive truth from the clash of white-hatted and black-hatted partisans. That approach barely distinguishes college campuses from public parks. We should ask students to join a community for whose members speech is not a weapon to deploy against the enemy, but the means by which people who pursue the truth and hope to live according to what they capture of it teach and learn from each other. The members of such a community may or may not turn out to be free speech warriors. But because they benefit from a diversity of opinion and depend on the freedom to follow arguments where they lead, they may prove more deeply attached to campus free speech than those who know only the standard free speech arguments.

In the fifth chapter, I use the debate over Israel in the academy as a case study. I began to write about higher education and the campus wing of the Boycott, Divestment, and Sanctions (BDS) movement at around the same time. I came to the Israel question through the back door, not as a pro-Israel man but as a concerned academic, convinced that the influence of BDS, whether one loves or despises Israel, compromises the missions of our colleges and universities. I see the BDS fight as closely connected to the issues raised in the other chapters. Other movements—the Palestinian issue was only a small part of the protests that swept through American campuses in 2015— would make fine case studies, but there is much to be said for dealing with what one knows best. Reflecting on how leading BDS advocates think of universities and their work there, and on the various ways in which BDS detractors have tried to combat it, will help us better understand why it can be difficult to do the work of becoming reasonable on our campuses, and how it can be done nonetheless.

That will be a bridge to my conclusion, in which I reflect briefly on prospects for reform.

The Closing of the American Mind was "written from the perspective of a teacher." The case for liberal education has been damaged by overuse of the term, as if it's a perfume one dabs on preprofessional degrees to make them more presentable, or a mandated kid's trip to the museum to absorb "culture." Liberal education is hard to describe, but it's connected to a vivid teacher's vision, the "divination" that "there is a human nature, and that assisting its fulfillment is [our] task," that "students are only potential, but [that] potential points beyond itself; and this is the source of the hope, almost always disappointed but ever renascent, that man is not just a creature of accident, chained to and formed by the particular cave in which he is born."[35] Understanding human nature and aiding in its fulfillment is a goal that is both unavoidable and just out of reach for people who care about young people. This problem, which would seem to require our undivided attention, is a problem from which we've become distracted.

My aim is to make us focus on it.

CHAPTER TWO

Left, Right, Wrong

Politics makes most of us stupid. It moves even those who aren't stupid to say stupid things. Alexander Hamilton, in opening *The Federalist Papers*, observes that "a torrent of angry and malignant passions will be let loose" in "cases of great national discussion." In that same opening, Hamilton accuses his opponents of conspiring, out of selfishness or "perverted ambition," to break the new country apart. Yet many of those opponents merely demanded a Bill of Rights, which the 1787 Constitution lacked. *The Federalist Papers* are among the most rational interventions into politics ever written. But even they remind us that to win in politics, we have to twist the views of our rivals and appeal to unworthy impulses. *The Federalist Papers*, even as they suggest that conserving the Founding means conserving a republic established by "reflection and choice," also suggest that it means maintaining a keen sense of reason's vulnerability in a storm.[1]

My students have heard that the debates between Abraham Lincoln and Stephen Douglas are the peak of American political discourse. When they read them, they're surprised to find each speaker spinning conspiracy theories in order to paint the other as, to coin a phrase, the enemy of the people. That doesn't mean that the Lincoln-Douglas Debates are overrated, or that politics is altogether irrational. It does mean that it's difficult to make room for rational arguments in politics, even in democracies that pride themselves on their relative enlightenment.

So, colleges and universities, if they are to be homes of reason, should be leery of politics. But they aren't.

More than fifty years ago, the authors of the Port Huron Statement, a founding document of American student activism, called for "an alliance of students and faculty" to galvanize a new left, taking in "allies in labor, civil rights, and other liberal forces outside the campus." Within the universities, this alliance would "consciously build a base for [its] assault upon the loci of power." From "its schools and colleges across the nations," a "militant left might awaken its allies." On this view, politics is not an extracurricular activity but the very stuff of higher education.[2]

Regardless of what you may have heard, our universities aren't governed by balding radicals and their student disciples. But today, the student activists of the sixties are heroes to many, and even administrators, those squares, usually profess to view activism as a sign of health. At least the kids are passionate about something. Seen in the right light, planning assaults on the loci of power, which has historically involved reading and the use of big words, looks like a rich alternative to beer pong.

It's telling that Richard Rorty, one of the most perceptive critics of the New Left that the Port Huron Statement helped launch, endorses its understanding of campuses as "centers of social protest." All "universities worthy of the name" have been such centers, and if "American universities ever cease to be such centers, they will lose both their self-respect and the respect of the learned world." Rorty contemns "conservative critics" who object to seizing universities as bases for assaults on the loci of

power. Such duffers disapprove of "politicizing" the universities. But as far as Rorty is concerned, if you visit a university,
and all you see is deep thinking going on, you're supposed to
shake your head, sniff, and say, "That's all fine and good, but
why no marching?"

Rorty, then, is mystified that any serious person objects to
left-wing activism as an aim of higher education. Such a person
ought to be "ashamed" of himself, for if universities aren't in the
business of remedying American sadism and selfishness, what
are the damned things for?[3] The debate on the left is not about
whether universities should be leery of politics, but rather over
what kind of politics they should enthusiastically embrace.

And the only debate in higher education is the debate on
the left.

Our Far Left-Liberal Universities

In *Passing on the Right: Conservative Professors in the Progressive
University,* Jon Shields and Joshua Dunn introduce a "closeted"
conservative professor who insists on meeting them at an off-
campus park. They find a "secluded spot," but their man "was
edgy and spoke softly." When "the sound of footsteps intruded
on our sanctuary, he stopped talking altogether, his eyes darting
about." This professor, on the job for ten years, was terrified of
being exposed as a conservative.[4]

At nonsectarian private colleges like mine, according to the
2016–17 Higher Education Research Institute Faculty Survey,
just 10.7% of professors consider themselves conservative, and
another 0.5% say they're on the far right. We're outnumbered
by the 13.8% of faculty who put themselves on the far left, not
to speak of the 50.5% who consider themselves liberals. Even if
you combine "middle of the road" faculty with self-identified

conservatives and far-rightists, that combination is still greatly outnumbered by the far left-liberal contingent, 64.3% to 35.7%. At all institutions surveyed, that disparity is 59.8% to 40.2%.[5]

In fields in which politics are most likely to be discussed—the relative parity of conservatives in engineering is cold comfort—things get still worse. In the social sciences, where my department of politics sits, John Kerry, who lost the presidential election of 2004, would have won it in a historic landslide, 88% to 6%.[6] I suppose I should rejoice that political science, according to a 2018 study of faculty at top liberal arts colleges, has only 8.2 registered Democrats for every registered Republican. The study didn't spot any Republicans in its sample of anthropologists.[7]

Yet most professors aren't sweating these numbers. According to Neil Gross, author of *Why Are Professors Liberal and Why Do Conservatives Care*, the most popular explanation among professors for the scarcity of conservative faculty is that conservatives are closed-minded. Closed-minded people aren't comfortable in higher education because people in higher education are so open-minded. The second most popular explanation is that conservatives "are too interested in making money to want jobs as professors." Higher education isn't exactly where the money is, and conservatives are—am I right?—all about the Benjamins.

One might expect that academics on the left, ever on the prowl for hidden prejudices, might find the near-total absence of conservatives in some departments troubling. But a lot of them consider the absence a natural and happy result of the backwardness and greed of conservatives. That, in this judgment, they may be relying on "strongly held stereotypes about liberals and conservatives" seems not to have entered their minds.[8]

Life at Left-Liberal Colleges and Universities

How does the overwhelming left-liberalism of our colleges and universities manifest itself? If you have enough interest in higher education to read this book, you know that even left-liberal professors, like Erika Christakis of Yale University, or Brett Weinstein of Evergreen State University, can spark protests merely by crossing students and colleagues somewhat further to the left.[9] You might think that actual conservatives who open their mouths can expect to be fired, if they're fortunate enough to avoid being boiled in oil.

But that hasn't been my experience. Because I studied with professors reputed to be conservatives, I couldn't, even were I so inclined, pass as a man of the left. Although it took me a while to secure a permanent position, I interviewed for several plum positions. If the deck were completely stacked against conservatives, I wouldn't have had the opportunity to bomb those interviews. My work for conservative outlets commenced before I earned tenure. Yet I can think of only one colleague over two decades who has treated me unprofessionally for political reasons. I've worked with hundreds of people. I doubt the percentage of difficult co-workers I've encountered in higher education is any higher than it would have been in another line of work.

My own good experience doesn't mean that conservatives are making it up when they complain about discrimination in the academy. It would be naïve, given a natural human weakness for tribalism, to think that political prejudices never influence tenure and hiring decisions. There are surely entire fields, like gender studies, in which the espousal of conservative views could deal a mortal blow to one's career. Moreover, there is some survey evidence that significant minorities of liberals and conservatives are willing to discriminate against their opposite numbers in hiring and other decisions.[10] Since liberals vastly outnumber conservatives in academia, conservatives must be bearing the brunt of whatever political discrimination may be occurring there.

Even when conservatives face no discrimination in hiring and promotion, universities can turn up the heat on them, particularly on social conservatives like Scott Yenor, who made the mistake of arguing, in a conservative outlet, that transgender activists want to weaken the rights of parents. For this, he was publicly accused, by the school's director of Diversity and Inclusion, of harboring a "pathetic fear" of change and of initiating a line of thought that ends in genocide.[11] Posters appeared on campus demanding that Yenor be fired, there were calls for him to be investigated, and the faculty senate entertained a resolution that would have amounted to a censure of their colleague. In fairness to Boise State, Yenor was not investigated, censured, or fired. But he was wrung out.[12]

Still, I'm not the only conservative who gets on all right in academia. According to Shields and Dunn, the conservative academics they interviewed "generally told us that the academy is far more tolerant than right-wing critics of the progressive university seem to imagine." Only about a third of their interviewees tried to hide their politics prior to earning tenure, tenure being a near-guarantee against being fired. That sounds like a lot, but given the high stakes involved, and the possibility that offending a vindictive colleague might sink one's chances, junior professors are notoriously cautious. They pretend the department chairperson's jokes are funny, that they love serving on committees, that the new strategic plan is a gem and, in sum, that everything is terrific. These are people inclined to conceal their very personalities, let alone their politics. So it's reassuring that the great majority of conservatives whom Shields and Dunn interviewed felt no need to hide.[13]

We should view these results with some skepticism. Interviewees willingly identified themselves as conservatives to Shields and Dunn, who don't claim their sample is representative. The professors who so identified themselves may be more content than other conservatives who didn't, perhaps for fear of being shunned or otherwise harmed. Yet Samuel Abrams, working with a much larger sample, and with a survey in which respondents remained anonymous, found that conservative professors are somewhat more satisfied in academia than liberals are.[14] Faced with such findings, critics of the liberal academy resort to "false consciousness" explanations of a sort usually more popular with the left. Conservatives in academia are so oppressed they've started to like it.[15]

This line of analysis, I'm sorry to say to my conservative brothers and sisters, is the last resort of the evidence-deprived.

We Don't Want No Trouble

But don't worry, friends. It's bad enough at colleges and universities. That small group on the far left, even if its members don't usually threaten the livelihoods of the few conservatives they work with, has an outsized influence on many campuses.

You've all seen a movie or TV show in which a character, sensing danger, raises his hands, takes a step back and says, "I don't want no trouble." To understand the influence of the left at our colleges and universities, you have to understand that most people who study or work at them don't want no trouble.

We faculty members don't want no trouble. We're at universities because we want to investigate interesting questions,

whether they concern dark matter or Aristotle. We like to be
around other odd birds who pursue such questions. Often, having been inspired by teachers, we like to mentor students.
Often, we get to do our work without much interference from
fellow teachers or higher-ups and are happiest when we're not
in each other's business. If a situation arises that requires us to
be in each other's business, particularly if people seem angry
about it, many of us will be tempted to appease whichever faction is capable of making the most trouble. Then we can get
back to our labs and offices.

Students don't want no trouble either. Although there are pe-
riods in which student activism is a popular sideline, few students
come to college to do politics. They may be there to get a job, or
to enjoy themselves before they have to get a job; most of them
hope to learn something. Some of them find activists irritating,
but for the most part, like their professors, students confronted
with a tense campus environment want to defuse the tension,
which means appeasing the people who are shouting loudest.

In a superb essay on how comedians are selected to perform
at college campuses, Caitlin Flanagan profiles the students,
members of activities committees, who help make the decisions. They're not usually activists themselves. But they're nice
people, unlikely to be deaf to students who say their feelings are
hurt, or that they feel threatened, by edgy jokes. And they're
cautious. So, although they may have "nuanced opinions" about
comedy, they understand that if you hire a comedian who hugs
the line between funny and offensive, there could be trouble.
Consequently, without much conviction, they choose "comedy
so thoroughly scrubbed of barb and aggression that if the most
hypersensitive weirdo on campus mistakenly wandered into a
performance, the words he would hear would fall on him like
a soft rain."[16]

Administrators, the main villains in Flanagan's tale, seriously don't want no trouble. Their job is to attract and retain students. They also don't want anything to unsettle the digestion of their alumni, who may not open their wallets if their stomachs are upset by scenes for which the curated annual report has left them unprepared. Yale will survive the viral video of a student screaming at a faculty member because his spouse was judged soft on offensive Halloween costumes. But most administrators don't work at universities that have $25 billion endowments and applicants willing to cut off a limb to be admitted. So most administrators would ban Halloween if they could. Short of that, they'll do what they can to stop students from getting upset about anything, especially in public. That means that their first impulse—also their second and third—is to appease those most likely to make trouble.

A mentor taught me, referring to our department, that anyone who cared about departmental affairs could have a disproportionate influence over them, because most department members, like the faculty I describe above, wanted to do their work without being bothered. The same is true of college campuses in general, and that helps explain why, even though the far left is a small minority on most campuses, far-leftists have an outsized influence. They care a lot about governing the college. They're more likely than other faculty members to describe themselves as "scholar-activists," meaning that, for them, as for the Port Huron gang, universities are primarily sites for doing political work. Whereas most faculty members consider academic governance a chore akin to weeding in the hot sun, for the scholar-activist, it's how you make universities more reflective of and effective at promoting your political priorities.

Jacques Berlinerblau, a credible witness in part because he denies that left-wing professors indoctrinate their students, agrees that those same professors have an influence well beyond their numbers. On an average campus, says Berlinerblau, there's a "tiny cohort of conservatives," a "much larger but graying and listless group of traditional liberals," and "a somewhat smaller *but much more institutionally influential and powerful* group of scholars on the extreme Left." Berlinerblau doesn't think that left-wing professors are interested in indoctrinating undergraduates, mainly because they're not interested in teaching. But he thinks they're eager "to control institutions" and are "really good at playing this game." It is the fond desire of the "politicized professor" that "you could walk from one side of the campus to another and never find an alternative to his worldview."[17]

Neither activist students nor politicized professors have numbers. But a funny thing happens when their determination, and willingness to make trouble, interacts with the desire of most others at the university to dodge trouble. You get universities willing to make large concessions, in the curriculum, in hiring, and in day-to-day management, to their leftmost constituents.

The Campus Atmosphere in Conclusion

I've said both that many conservatives are comfortable on campus and that the far left has an outsized influence there. What, then, are campuses like? Conditions vary, but I have no reason to believe that the campuses where I've worked are unusual. Here's one telling episode.

I'm at an informal meeting about a first-year course, of which I teach a section. A student—one or two are present along with faculty—observes that the text we now use to discuss race isn't working. The other, benighted, kids aren't grasping the concept of white privilege, according to which our social and political arrangements not incidentally but systematically favor white people. Yes, systematic racial bias is the subject of the book in question, but students are still resisting the idea that they are personal beneficiaries of a system best described as oppressive. We need to choose a text that will do a better job of making sure our students get it. The student who makes this point—an excellent student by the way—hasn't learned that it's imprudent, even in today's academy, to propose that our aim as teachers is to cram our point of view through the clenched jaws of our students.

But no one says anything. So I say that, in this particular course, we're trying to teach students how to reflect on fundamental questions, like what justice is, rather than to break down their resistance to critical race theory. I say that I've been teaching, in another course, a debate about race in America between Ta Nehisi Coates of *The Atlantic* and Jonathan Chait of *New York Magazine*. According to the latter, although we are far from racial equality, the basic story of the United States is of "halting, non-continuous, but clear improvement."[18] According to the former, "white supremacy" is our heritage and has only been "reinforced," repeatedly, since the end of chattel slavery.[19] I say that we are now being asked to construct a curriculum that will cause students to reject Chait, not to mention black intellectuals who share his view, and to embrace Coates. I conclude that this means that the college, in a required course, will not only be attempting to push students to the left but also telling them precisely where they should sit on the spectrum of left-liberal opinion. I await a motion to make me professor of the week.

Instead, another faculty member, a shade or two whiter than I am, announces that my arguments are a symptom of "white anxiety."

After waiting in vain for support, I object that accusing one's opponents, without a shred of evidence, of being in the grips of a race-based mental illness, is no way to advance our understanding of an issue about which, after all, reasonable people disagree.

Awkward silence. Someone changes the subject.

What can we learn from this incident? Let me begin with what it doesn't suggest. It doesn't suggest that left-wing ideologues run our campuses. In this course, as in every other required first-year course I've taught, we continued to read a variety of texts, many of them the kinds of classics some conservatives believe are no longer taught at the university. Nearly all of my colleagues would nod vigorously if told that our mission is not to indoctrinate our students but to introduce them to influential and worthy approaches to enduring questions. And, in spite of my public outing as an anxious white dude, I wasn't frogmarched out of my office the next day and packed off to reeducation camp, or even unfriended on Facebook.

What the incident does suggest is that most faculty members, whether or not they accept certain pieties of the left, don't question them aloud. So it's easier and less controversial to assert that we live in a white supremacist culture than it is to question that assertion. It's easier and less controversial to assert that we live in a culture that endorses rape than it is to question that assertion. It's easier and less controversial to assert that we should revamp our academic programming to advance racial and gender justice than it is to question that assertion. It's easier and less controversial to admit to a vote for Jill Stein than it is to admit to a vote for George W. Bush. And, finally, it's easier to sit silently when one's colleagues are, without evidence, accused of harboring a racial bias so deep that it infects their every argument than it is to object. We should worry about self-censorship (though people shouldn't blurt out everything that's on their minds) not only for its immediate but also its long-term consequences. As my father-in-law, the political theorist Werner Dannhauser, wrote, "What is unsayable becomes unthinkable for most human beings."[20]

It may seem odd to say both that most faculty members I know reject the idea that our mission is to indoctrinate our students and that it's hard to question the idea that our academic programming should advance a left-wing conception of social justice. This situation defies logic. But, in my experience, the leading solution to the problem that turning colleges into social justice Sunday schools contradicts what most professors otherwise think about their missions is not to talk about it.

Did I mention that we don't want no trouble?

I was discussing a curricular proposal with a liberal friend of mine, an excellent teacher and no ideologue. The proposal was surprisingly forthright about its intent, which was to move students toward a certain understanding of justice and inspire them to act on it. My friend planned to vote for it. He was convinced that few professors would teach the proposed text in the spirit the proposers hoped it would be taught. Moreover, although he wasn't the sort to push a point of view on his students, he didn't think that it would be a calamity if some professors indulged themselves that way, so long as that point of view was antiracist.

That suggests an additional explanation, admittedly speculative, of why highly contestable views aren't challenged vigorously on our campuses. Remember Berlinerblau's graying traditional liberals? They may have supported President Obama while their more radical colleagues saw him as a neoliberal, drone-war-waging, sellout. But even grayer and more moderate people of the left have sympathy for the young and radical. They may worry a little that their colleagues are undermining the devotion of colleges and universities to inquiry, a devotion they themselves share. But that worry competes with the sense that the young are usually on the right side of history.

Whatever the best explanation of the causes may be, it seems safe to say this about the political atmosphere on many college campuses. Although conservatives, for the most part, can work in peace, and although not that many faculty members are on the far left, there is little appetite for challenging conventional left-wing wisdom. The problem is not that left-wing activists are wrong, and everyone else is right. The former can compel the latter to reexamine views—about what educators should be doing, or about how service workers should be treated, or about how the United States should conduct itself abroad—that deserve scrutiny and may have hardened into prejudices. The problem is, rather, that the public discourse at many of our colleges and universities, a public discourse that is bound to influence decisions about curriculum, hiring, student life, and other matters, approximates in some subject areas the discourse of a one-party state.

What's Wrong with Being Politicized?

Nowadays, if you complain to a professor that colleges and universities are politicized, you may be met with a condescending smile. The jaded have the politician's habit of dismissing charges, once proven, as old news. But even among the earnest, the view that academic work can be anything other than political seems naïve. I tried, years back, to persuade a colleague of mine on the left to co-write a letter concerning the Boycott, Divestment, and Sanctions movement (BDS), which I'll discuss in chapter 5. We agreed that in the name of a dubious and hyperpartisan understanding of Middle East politics, BDS activists seek to drive certain institutions and individuals out of the community of scholars. We agreed that this position, where it prevails, threatens academic freedom.

But my colleague balked when I suggested we criticize BDS for dragging universities into politics. I wanted to argue that if we concede that colleges and universities are properly vehicles for people's politics, legislators and trustees are free to conclude that they, and not professors, should get to decide what politics gets taught. This point still seems to me almost too obvious to need stating. But, my colleague asked rhetorically, aren't colleges and universities inherently political? And don't scholars always bring to the table a politics that guides the questions they ask and the conclusions they draw?

What does it mean to worry that our universities are politicized? Our worry can't be that professors have motives for entering academic life other than the ice-cold pursuit of the truth. No one blames the biology researcher who wants not only to inquire into the natural world but also to cure cancer. A friend of mine who went into the field of security studies traces his interest back to the Yom Kippur War, which he saw unfold on television when he was four years old. There's nothing wrong with entering the security studies field in the hope of promoting peace. While there are pure researchers who select an object of study for no reason apart from intellectual curiosity, we don't need to demand such purity of our researchers or teachers. But we can ask them, as members of a scholarly community, to agree with this proposition: in conflicts between one's convictions and the best argument, the best argument should prevail.

To worry that our universities are politicized can't mean, either, that when we become convinced in the course of our work of a politically relevant conclusion, we must remain silent about it. Prudence counsels academics to be wary of being perceived as partisans. But there's no principled reason that an economist who, after rigorous study, concludes that the minimum wage will or won't depress employment, should refrain from sharing that conclusion in an op-ed, or even at a political convention.

And our worry can't mean that we think naïvely that colleges and universities can be insulated completely from politics. In balking at the idea that politicization is our enemy, my colleague on the left may have been recalling the feminist slogan, "The personal is the political." Arrangements deemed private—for example how husbands should treat wives—can't be addressed without attention to arrangements deemed public—who rules and to what end? Feminists or not, we conservatives can hardly object to the commonsense idea that politics, even liberal democratic politics, has far-reaching effects on how we think about and act within families, neighborhoods, businesses, and yes, universities. Similarly, one can't deny that colleges and universities are political in the narrow sense of involving relations of power—between administrators, faculty, and students, between the tenured and non-tenured, between men and women, and so on. Those relations of power can undermine the university as a community of people who are trying to be reasonable, in which one's status should depend on one's capacity to make and judge arguments well.

Rather, we who worry about the politicization of our universities take issue with the idea that there's no such thing as a common good among truth-seekers, which we should prefer to our partisan convictions and use to clear away the prejudices and distortions introduced by politics. We're not convinced by the philosopher Michel Foucault, who puts truth in quotation marks and claims that it is "linked in a circular relation with systems of power."[21] We're convinced instead by the historian,

Thomas Haskell, who argues that if we adopt Foucault's premises, then assertions about academic freedom, about the special
status professors merit by virtue of their devotion to the truth,
has "to be interpreted as self-serving rhetoric."[22] We're surprised that our colleagues think that they can adopt such premises and still have a leg to stand on if politicians say, "Since you
admit that your enterprise is just another means of exercising
power, and since you're weak and we're strong, we're removing
you and installing our people in your place."

What could they do other than shrug, smile, and say "You've
got us."?

That practical concern aside, the slogan "Everything is political" simplifies and diminishes intellectual work. Go back to that
informal meeting about a first-year course, in which my colleagues and I were discussing what to include regarding race.
Thirty years ago, the discussion would have been about "multiculturalism." Back then, an earnest, moderate, philosophical
liberal might argue to include, say, Du Bois's *The Souls of Black
Folk*, by appealing to a sensible idea: the careful investigation of
diverse peoples and civilizations is part of what's needed to become reasonable.[23] Such investigation reveals alternatives to
our habitual way of looking at things and causes us to wonder
if what we think reasonable is, in truth, narrow-minded. Without it, "Be reasonable!" can be less a call to open one's mind
than to close it. Du Bois pursues this theme when he proposes
that the "rich and bitter depth" of the American black experience can give America and the world "new points of view."[24]

Allan Bloom argued that, whatever earnest liberal philosophers might say, multiculturalism was made popular by political
considerations. Its intention was to "propagandize acceptance
of different ways," not promote understanding of those ways.[25]
Whether Bloom was right, as I think, or not, one is today more

likely to say forthrightly that "diversity" in the curriculum is needed not to investigate peoples or cultures in the hope of becoming more reasonable but to uncover power and privilege in order to overturn them. For this purpose, it's probably more useful to read and reread Peggy McIntosh's "White Privilege: Unpacking the Invisible Knapsack" than to read Du Bois. McIntosh may be white, but she deals exclusively with the central issue, oppression, and fulfills directly the aim of education, to cause holders of skin or sex privilege to recognize that they're oppressors and to inspire them to reject oppressive power structures.[26]

Du Bois, a keen analyst of power and an activist, is no stranger to this species of argument. But you might say he sometimes got sidetracked by other concerns. In particular, he entertains the idea of a "sovereign human soul that seeks to know itself and the world about it," that has a good in common with other would-be knowers, that imagines itself in communion with Shakespeare and Aristotle, and supposes it can be "wed with Truth."[27]

That sounds more interesting to me than "everything is political," but people engaged in serious activism don't have the luxury of being interesting.

Undermining Our Mission: Curriculum

Protesters shutting down speeches or shouting at professors make good video. But the consequences of the situation I've outlined, in which professors, administrators, and students let the pieties of the left go unquestioned, are subtler. I'll focus on those consequences that bear directly on the mission of the university, to help students become reasonable people, and to nurture in them the understanding that anyone who claims to be reasonable must yield to the best arguments.

Back to the curriculum. In 2015, the faculty of Columbia University's required Literature Humanities class (LitHum) voted to add Toni Morrison's *Song of Solomon* to the syllabus. As Julie Crawford, then chair of LitHum, observed, *Song of Solomon* was "the first work by a living author on the syllabus, the first by an American, and the first by a black American." Crawford reflects on the puzzling but characteristic way in which the discussion of Morrison was framed by some commentators: "The inclusion of Morrison increased the 'diversity' of the course, and, in particular, ... she [was] the first writer 'of color' on the syllabus."

By diversity, no one meant "range of experience and expression." Students in LitHum are expected to make sense of texts that emerged from the "Mediterranean and Near East" 2,800 years ago. They're expected to decipher texts from "fourth-century Roman North Africa, fourteenth-century Florence," and "nineteenth-century St. Petersburg." They're expected to enter the minds of authors who, though they sometimes knew of each other, come from bewilderingly different worlds, speak different languages, understand what it means to be human in deeply different ways, and articulate their understandings in distinctive forms of poetry and prose. Yet "diversity" as used by champions of the change was really "shorthand for meaningful categories in current American political discourse." Only in these terms would reading Toni Morrison, an American author whose America we inhabit, count as an experience of diversity more than reading Homer, whose world is almost lost to us. But Homer is white.

Except he isn't, as Crawford points out. Nor, in "any meaningful sense," are St. Augustine, the "early scribes of Genesis" or a number of other writers read in LitHum. One doesn't need color photographs of the various authors to understand Crawford's point, that "whiteness is not a transhistorical category" and that "what we call race . . . has not worked in the same way, or been understood in the same way, across time or culture."[28]

If you doubt that, consider Sarah E. Bond's 2017 article, "Why We Need to Start Seeing the Classical World in Color." Bond, a classicist, begins by observing that "many of the statues, reliefs, and sarcophagi created in the ancient Western world were in fact painted." The association of classical sculpture with white marble conveys a "false idea of homogeneity—everyone was very white!—across the Mediterranean region." Bond argues that this false idea of "white" Greeks and Romans contributes to "the false construction of Western civilization as white." And that idea makes it artificially difficult for people of color to "see themselves in the ancient landscape that we present to them."[29] For making this scholarly and only mildly political argument in an online arts journal, Bond found herself subjected to violent threats, emanating from the right.[30]

In insisting that Western civilization is dead, white, and male, the alt-right and much of the left are united. Who says bipartisanship is dead?

Those who today speak for curricular diversity in terms the alt-right finds congenial demand that we think of the disparate authors of the so-called Western canon as "dead white males." They demand of colleagues, administrators, and the students whose minds they're charged with improving, that they bow to bad arguments, that they pretend not to know things that they know in order to be on the right side of contemporary politics. They demand that we say with a straight face that it's more of a challenge to our beliefs to read a twenty-first-century lesbian, or African American, or Latino, or disabled person (not a Jew, though—Jews are riding high), than it is to read Homer or Montaigne, with whom we have less in common. That is to say,

they demand that we demean ourselves and disserve our students by presenting propaganda as wisdom.

Undermining Our Mission: Student Mental Health

A similar demand influences our discussion of "microaggressions."[31] Microaggressions are offenses, generally unintentional,
against members of disadvantaged groups. They range from
minor—"So, you're black; is Beyoncé authentic?"—to major—
"I've never met an articulate black person before; how did you
escape the hood mentality?" Microaggressions have been part of
mainstream thinking for only a decade or so, but campuses are
already hurriedly implementing programs to stamp them out.[32]

Few deny that words can cause great harm. But it's a long way
from this premise to the conclusion that a class of insults called
microaggressions should be exposed and eradicated. In 2017,
Perspectives on Psychological Science published a review of research on microaggressions by Scott Lilienfeld, a professor of
psychology at Emory University. Lilienfeld's review found the
research wanting. For one thing, it's hard to say what a microaggression is, which makes microaggressions difficult to study.
Was it a microaggression when, one day, two of my Protestant
friends shared their concern that, because I was Jewish, I'd be
going to hell? I didn't take it that way, though today I suppose I
might be encouraged to report it to a bias response team.[33]
What if someone says, "I believe that the most qualified person
should get the job regardless of race"? That sounds innocuous
but is regarded as a microaggression in "widely used training
materials," presumably because it denies, by suggesting color-
blindness is possible, the pervasiveness of racism.[34] Perhaps
one shouldn't lump together the various phenomena that fall

under the name "microaggression," and a research program bound to a category so "imprecisely defined and porous in its boundaries" is suspect. Before we draw firm conclusions, "it will be essential to shore up the microaggression concept considerably."[35]

Lilienfeld finds little or no support for the fundamental premises of programs that target microaggressions. We don't know whether or not "microaggressions reflect implicitly prejudicial and implicitly aggressive motives."[36] There's not much evidence that "microaggressions are interpreted negatively by most or all minority group members" or even that microaggressions "exert an adverse impact on the mental health of recipients; researchers have uncovered correlations but not a causal relationship between microaggressions and "adverse mental health outcomes."[37] Moreover, Lilienfeld thinks that programs designed to help with microaggressions may make matters worse for students. A "heightened attention to microaggressions may sensitize minority individuals to subtle signs of potential prejudice, leading them to become hypervigilant." They may "become more likely to experience negative psychological reactions following minor perceived provocations." The psychologist, Jonathan Haidt, and the free speech activist, Greg Lukianoff, have raised a similar issue about the related phenomenon of "trigger warnings," meant to alert students to the potential trauma to which different readings and activities might subject them. "People acquire their fears not just from their own past experiences, but from social learning as well. If everyone around you acts as though something is dangerous— elevators, certain neighborhoods, novels depicting racism— then you are at risk of acquiring that fear too."[38]

In light of all this, there's a good case for one of Lilienfeld's suggestions: that we halt microaggression programs until we're confident they're doing more good than harm. But in a response to Lilienfeld, Derald Wing Sue, a pioneer in microaggression research, inadvertently indicates why colleges are unlikely to do so: it would be ideologically unacceptable. Sue doesn't try to contest Lilienfeld's review; instead, he suggests that science is not the right framework in which to consider the issue. Microaggression programs are about "experiential reality and about listening to the voices of those most oppressed." Those in the privileged majority may "enjoy the luxury of waiting for proof," but proof must not be demanded of those who aren't privileged. Lilienfeld is callously "applying the principle of *skepticism* to the study of microaggressions, which may unintentionally dilute, dismiss, and negate the lived experience of marginalized groups."[39] Consider again the possibility that the aim of education is to promote reason and to form human beings who think it a disgrace not to listen to it. Sue and others who insist on microaggression programs, even when confronted with reasons to think such programs might hurt those they are designed to help, propose that marginalized students mustn't be taught to question their subjective experiences. Faculty members must pretend that the arguments in favor of microaggression trainings are stronger than they are. This posture, apart from humiliating everyone involved, is antithetical to the mission of the university.

Undermining Our Mission: Education as Exorcism

Toward the beginning of this chapter, I referred to a debate on the left concerning what kind of politics universities should embrace. But it was an exaggeration to call it a debate. What Richard Rorty called the cultural left was already the main left on campus when he identified it more than two decades ago. That cultural left sees the enemy as above all a mind-set that infects our very language. The causes of cruelty toward blacks, women, the disabled, and other historically disadvantaged groups are deep in our culture and can only be rectified by a kind of revolution, in which the regime to be overthrown is not a monarchy or oligarchy but the whitecisheteropatriarchy. Therefore, unlike what Rorty calls the reform left, which tended to focus on elections and economic change, the cultural left focuses on getting at a problem, sometimes dubbed "power," that has infiltrated everything. Power in this sense, as Rorty vividly puts it, "has left an indelible stain on every word in our language and on every institution in our society. It is always already there and cannot be spotted coming or going." It is "as much inside one as outside one" and "only interminable individual and social analysis . . . can help us escape from the infinitely fine meshes of its invisible web."[40]

Since reason and the norms that govern debate are themselves infected by power, whose "ubiquity is reminiscent of the ubiquity of Satan," it's no surprise that commentators, not all of them right-wingers, compare the academic left to a religious orthodoxy. "If you happen to see the world in a different way," Andrew Sullivan says sarcastically, "if you're a liberal or libertarian or even, gasp, a conservative, if you believe that a university is a place where any idea, however loathsome, can be debated and refuted, you are not just wrong, you are immoral." Dissenters, who might "contaminate others' souls," must be converted or crushed. "You can't reason with heresy."[41]

Consider the cancellation of classes at Connecticut College, one day in March 2015, because of a series of incidents that, though some were disturbing, might occur in any community of non-saints. In August 2014, a professor of philosophy, Andrew Pessin, wrote a Facebook post on the Israeli-Palestinian conflict that, when it was made public, offended and angered some students. The post, which was carelessly worded, could be read as comparing Palestinians to dogs, though, read in context, it applied, without question, only to Hamas terrorists.

Pessin was denounced by some students as a racist. More strikingly, despite the ambiguity of what Pessin had written, and his subsequent apology, several academic departments, including history, sociology, and theater, stepped forward to "condemn speech that is full of bigotry and hate."[42] There followed exchanges on the then-popular anonymous forum Yik Yak, in which Pessin's critics were targets of nasty criticism themselves, and in which anti-Semitic epithets were deployed (Pessin is Jewish). The college responded to all this by holding a forum. Administrators canceled early evening "events, programs, and practices" to support the forum, which reportedly became a three-hour-long airing of student grievances concerning racism.[43]

But that one forum, and the cancellation of events to allow as many as possible to attend it, was deemed insufficient. A new incident, according to a letter from President Katherine Bergeron, of "racist graffiti" had been uncovered. This was an emergency: "We must take action immediately to expose and eradicate this ignorance and hatred." A mere three-hour forum wouldn't do the trick. Bergeron had "decided to cancel [the next day's] classes to ensure these events receive the proper attention."[44] Ultimately, Pessin left Connecticut College on medical leave and didn't return until more than two years had passed. They never did catch the racist graffiti artist, who likely was not a member of the campus community.[45]

Without downplaying the pressure Bergeron must have been under, or the agitation on campus over troubling events, I think that Bergeron's decision to cancel an entire day of classes over bathroom graffiti is hard to defend. Even authoritarian regimes have trouble keeping a lid on graffiti and even good communities are unlikely to eradicate anonymous, ugly expression. What message does it send to declare a state of campus emergency over such incidents and to cancel all college business in the hopeless hope of eradicating, as one might seek to exorcise demons, the last racist graffiti artists? While I wouldn't describe this as the beginning of a trend, I would describe it as the logical culmination of a view according to which one of the primary purposes of a college campus is to encourage left political activism. In that case, the task of cultivating reason, itself inhabited by demonic prejudices, properly takes a back seat to the task of exorcism.

No wonder that St. Olaf College, in spring 2017, prompted by a racist note and subsequent protests, canceled classes. It may seem cynical to suggest that administrators, by handling incidents of racism this way, empower anyone who cares to shut down a campus.

However, the St. Olaf note was a hoax.[46]

Burn It Down: The Conservative Response

If the campus left has been, in the face of great challenges to colleges and universities, chasing the last racist graffiti artists, conservatives are tracking another strange quarry—the religious studies / gender studies double major.[47]

You see, somebody once did that double major and ended up in a lot of debt.

I first came across the name Cortney Munna in Glenn Reynolds's 2012 book *The Higher Education Bubble*.[48] Munna, twenty-six years old, was still $96,000 in debt for her New York University degree. She was making $22 per hour as a photographer.[49]

But the *New York Times* story that alerted commentators to Munna's plight was loan porn, not a serious treatment of student loan debt. Munna was a wildly unrepresentative case. In 2012, median student loan debt, for those who held it—many don't borrow—was $12,800.[50] The mean, to which loan worriers always appeal, was $23,300, brought up by the small percentage of borrowers who, like Munna, had racked up enormous debts.

But conservatives, even some who embrace the kind of conservatism I favor, found Munna irresistible. Reynolds himself founded and writes for the widely read blog *Instapundit*, and Munna's case was also taken up by well-known conservative figures, including George Will, Rod Dreher, and William Bennett. Perhaps one reason for the attention is that Munna was, as already noted, a religious studies / women's studies major. That's rich, right? Left-wing professors, like so many Snidely Whiplashes tying damsels to the train tracks, lure poor Munna into majoring in an impractical, highly politicized, humanities major, leaving her with a mountain of debt.

But Munna is wildly unrepresentative in large part because of her majors. Hardly anyone majors in women's studies. In 2014–15, 1,333 women's studies degrees were awarded throughout the country. That is 7/100 of 1% of the 1,894,000 degrees conferred that academic year. Approximately 4,500 were awarded in religious studies, Munna's second major. That's another 2/10 of 1%. Cortney Munna, her indebtedness and majors considered, was the rarest of rare birds. For those worried that colleges and universities are too into the humanities, bear in mind that business alone accounted in that same year for better than 19% of all degrees awarded. Health professions accounted for another 11.5% or so.[51] The idea that the problem in higher education is an overproduction of Cortney Munnas is laughably wrong.[52] So why are otherwise intelligent people making this case?

For one thing, Munna props up the "higher education bubble" idea that has won conservatives over. Tuition has increased at well above the rate of inflation (net price, what students pay after aid is factored in, has, however, steadied recently). At the same time, although college has become increasingly important for people who want to remain in the middle class, some college graduates find themselves unemployed and more find themselves underemployed. Under these circumstances, the argument goes, we can expect that parents and other education consumers will abandon all but the top brick-and-mortar colleges in favor of cheaper online options. Traditional colleges and universities, threatened, defend "existing interests" and look to fill their seats with paying customers, the good of students be damned. Innovative "edupunks" are heroes because they're "interested in finding new ways of teaching and learning" that will enable students to get a better education at a lower cost. Change is coming, "it is unlikely to be either modest or gradual," and those who wish to survive had better climb aboard the good ship Disruption.[53]

This story isn't as silly as the story that places Cortney Munna at the center of our higher education woes. But it's a little silly. It neglects the fact that upstarts, not traditional colleges, are at the heart of our recent student loan troubles and have thus far suffered the most serious consequences of deflation in the higher education sector. According to a Brookings Institute report, students attending for-profit institutions in 2011–12 borrowed just $848 less on average than students at private non-profits and $1,811 more than students at four-year public institutions. Attendees of for-profits tend to be less well-off than attendees of private non-profits, and they default on their loans at a much higher rate (almost triple in fiscal year 2010).[54] One might add that the recent history of for-profits has a bubbly feel. From 2000 to 2010, enrollment at for-profits nearly *quadrupled*, while, over the same period, enrollment at private non-profits increased at a much more modest 20%.[55] After 2010, the floor dropped out of the for-profit sector, whose enrollment declined by more than a third between 2010 and 2015 and has continued to decline.

It's true that, as a 2019 article puts it, "higher education enrollments have been falling for years" in the United States. Is this a sign of the bubble Reynolds predicted would soon burst? Signs point to no. The number of four-year private non-profits fell by about 1.2%, between 2015–16 and 2018–19, but there remained more such colleges and universities after that drop than there had been in 2009. Four-year for-profits fell nearly 49%, and there were 35.5% fewer of them than in 2009.[56]

Yes, many non-profit colleges and universities are under significant pressure now. And, because the college-aged population is projected to decline, they were already anticipating a bumpy ride even before the global pandemic, which is widely expected to make a challenging climate much worse. Bubble conservatives may at last get the closings they've longed for, if not for the reasons they've predicted.[57] But the higher education bubble, if we can speak of one at all, isn't a creature of irresponsible hidebound colleges that are being disrupted by innovators. It's the supposed innovators who best fit the description of irresponsible institutions signing up students who can't afford college and leaving them without the resources to pay off their loans.

So why have so many conservatives pushed a misleading story? You can understand the libertarian-leaning Reynolds being charmed by it: what libertarian doesn't cheer a fat, happy government suckling being outcompeted by scrappy punks? But even traditionalist conservatives, who ordinarily shake their canes at punks, have adopted the Reynolds line. One can only speculate about the motives of our bubblists, but my best guess is that they're in despair about higher education.

Consider Victor Davis Hanson, the renowned classicist and military historian. His approach to higher education is in many respects that of a traditionalist. Until recently, universities acted as "cultural custodians," and shaped "literate citizens," skilled readers, writers, and reasoners, who "appreciated the history of their civilization and understood the rights and responsibilities of their unique citizenship."[58] But the university "now finds itself being bypassed technologically, conceptually, and culturally, in ways both welcome and disturbing." Hanson, to his credit, acknowledges that the private, for-profit, largely online enterprises that compete with traditional higher education speed up a "creeping vocationalism," a single-minded emphasis on job skills that undermines classical education. Such schools bring more shovels with which to bury "the old notion of offering liberal arts classes to enrich citizenship."

That's the disturbing part of the bypassing of colleges and universities. However, inasmuch as brick-and-mortar colleges have all but ceded their cultural custodianship and liberal education missions in the face of the challenges from the left discussed earlier in this chapter, the upstarts certainly don't make matters worse. Their "unspoken premise is that if universities do not believe in the value of teaching Western civilization as part of a mandated general-education curriculum, then why not simply go to the heart of the matter and offer computer-programming skills or aeronautical-engineering know-how without the pretense of a broad education?"

In other words, if what we once called "liberal education" is now an empty promise, we may as well take our vocationalism straight, without the sermons. Things may blow up, then, for many conventional colleges, but—and here is the welcome part—"the Internet," "religious schools," and "CDs and DVDs" will increasingly provide places to go for those in need of a serious education. It may be regrettable that people will be forced to locate such sources amid a Wild West of education hawkers. It may be regrettable that they'll have to relearn how to operate their DVD players. But the American university has "forfeited the only commodity," the capacity to offer a classical education, "that made it irreplaceable." This "forfeited" tells you that although the struggle may continue over classical education, it has already been lost, so much so that Hanson has called the American university a "virtual outlaw institution," whose corrupt professors and administrators offer little of value and saddle clueless student-clients with unpayable debt.[59]

While Hanson isn't shouting "Burn, baby, burn," his argument does suggest that universities are so far gone that nothing short of a counter-revolution has a chance of helping them. His reasoning reminds me of Michael Anton's, which I introduced in the preface. Anton famously begins, "2016 is the Flight 93 election: charge the cockpit or you die. You may die anyway. You—or the leader of your party—may make it into the cockpit and not know how to fly or land the plane. There are no guarantees."[60] Anton goes on to argue, to exaggerate only somewhat, that since a few more years of Obama-style liberalism will destroy the country anyway, what the hell—let's roll the dice. Although there's more than one strain of conservative thought about our colleges and universities, we have, on the whole, entered into the "what the hell" phase of the enterprise.

It has not been ever thus. When William F. Buckley wrote *God and Man at Yale* in 1951, he thought, with many of today's conservatives, that universities were dominated by suspect professors. They were imposing secularism and the New Deal, rather than the convictions of a cultural left yet to be born, but imposing them nonetheless. Buckley also thought—as befits a man who would say that the *National Review* "stands athwart history, yelling Stop"—that the mission of university reform was a longshot. Yet, he gives us the twentieth-century intellectual, Arthur Koestler: "I . . . happen to believe in the ethical imperative of fighting evil, even if the fight is hopeless."[61] Buckley was a happy warrior, despite long odds. His prescription was not to cheer on the forces of creative destruction, in the unlikely, not particularly conservative, hope that someday, some way, something better might emerge out of the ashes. Rather, he urged university trustees to intervene with a view to restoring what Buckley saw as the core of the mission of the best universities, to preserve the best in the Western tradition.

Buckley's vision of universities as defenders of a kind of orthodoxy, though it leaves more room for inquiry than simplistic ideas of orthodoxy might acknowledge, contrasts sharply with Allan Bloom's idea, that "our chronic lack of certainty" about fundamental questions means that liberal education aims at "knowing the alternative answers" and "thinking about them." But for a time in the history of conservative thought, a fruitful alliance between these two positions emerged. A conservative like Buckley set out to defend known but unpopular truths. Such a conservative thought that relativism, a view according to which there are no truths, only the opinions of cultures and individuals, was a scourge. Bloom may have thought that the university should do no more than teach students to reflect on fundamental questions, to know the best alternative answers, and to follow the arguments wherever they might lead. But such a university, by virtue of taking Buckley's answers seriously, by giving them, as I said in the preface, a hearing, would be much better than the universities Buckley saw in front of him. Accordingly, Buckley's *National Review* published the Allan Bloom article that gave birth to *The Closing of the American Mind*, and Buckley gave Bloom his seal of approval when he hosted him on *Firing Line*. For a time, education understood as the cultivation of the knowledge and virtues essential to the pursuit of the truth and education understood primarily as the transmission and strengthening of known truths were allies against a relativistic left that denied both of these possibilities.

If today, conservatives, instead of standing athwart history yelling "Stop," are now stamping on the higher education bubble yelling "Pop," it must be because they believe, as Hanson seems to, that the battle of the universities has been lost and that the best policy is to burn them down, rather than leave them to our enemies. Perhaps we can return in a century or two to build again.

This hopelessness is unwarranted. Even today, a student attending the University of Wisconsin, Madison, which among public institutions has a strong left-wing reputation, can seek out the American Democracy Forum, a program devoted to the study of the American Founding and political thought more broadly. I doubt a Buckley would find much to quibble with there. Claremont McKenna College, the seat of some of the nastier student demonstrations of the recent past, houses the Salvatori Center, which "examines timeless truths in an effort to understand our civic condition."[62] From Harvard's Program in Constitutional Government to Roosevelt University's Montesquieu Forum, programs exist at numerous colleges and universities to support the study of old books and the pursuit of big questions.

Are we winning? No. Are we, and here I include professors from across the political spectrum who value liberal education, able to preserve that kind of education as a living, accessible, possibility for a great many students? Yes. Conservatives ought to spend less time drafting brilliant headlines about individual students, among the millions who attend college, who hold unfortunate views (*Campus Reform* once published an entire story about a single student who said something irritating about "manspreading") [63] and more time highlighting such successes. The old alliance between Buckley and Bloom needs reaffirming.

CHAPTER THREE

The Importance of Being
Reasonable

In the first chapter, I made gentle fun of defenders of liberal
education, like the Association of American Colleges and Universities, for sticking the liberal education label on a package of
buzzwords. But it's easy to make fun, harder to articulate a plausible account of liberal education. I take my shot in this
chapter.

The highest aim of liberal education is not a set of skills but
a kind of person. The liberally educated person says to herself,
following Locke, that there "cannot be anything . . . so misbecoming . . . anyone who pretends to be a rational creature, as
not to yield to plain reason and the conviction of clear arguments." This kind of person, who honors reason, still has to
work at becoming reasonable. The odds against reason are long.
But let's lean into our ambitions and call her a reasonable person.[1] What makes shaping reasonable people a better aim for
liberal educators than shaping people who deal well with complex ideas and situations, an aim frequently invoked by rele-
vance mongers?

On Smart People Who Are Stupid

To begin with, people who deal well with complexity are often also dopes. Yes, politics makes most of us stupid. But when we say that politics has made someone stupid, we have in mind a person who is otherwise smart. Rocket scientists, doctors, constitutional law theorists, and others, whose high capacity to deal with complex ideas can't be doubted, are, alas, the same people who appall us on Facebook and Twitter. The problem with your average social media nemesis isn't that he's bad at reasoning. He may be good at marshaling evidence for weak arguments and exposing weaknesses in strong arguments. He has all the tools to detect prejudices—in others—but doesn't turn those tools on himself. Like a spokesperson for a cornered politician, he identifies your exaggerations and errors, but does so in the name of a deeply partisan, perhaps delusional, view of things.

Obscured in our praise of liberal education for preparing students to confront a complex world is the difference between those who consider reason an instrument to get the better of others and those who consider reason an authority. The former are marked by their tendency to cling to their argument long after the evidence against it is decisive. If anything, they fight more aggressively after their case has crumbled. As we saw in the preface, when we exclaim, in frustration, "Be reasonable!" we don't mean, "Kindly observe the rules of deduction and induction with greater care." We may not even be aware of a specific error our tormentor has made. We mean, "Stop playing around, or trying to win, or serving your party, or selling your wares, and consider, as if it really mattered, what valid conclusions we can draw from what we know."

A vast psychological literature, usefully filtered through popular books like *Thinking Fast and Slow*,[2] counts some of the depressingly many ways in which educated people are biased. Knowledge, there's reason to believe, can make matters worse. Charles Taber and Milton Lodge, both political scientists, tested the hypothesis that "when given a chance to pick and choose what information to look at," people "will seek out sympathetic, nonthreatening sources." The hypothesis held up. People in favor of gun control or affirmative action, even when urged to be evenhanded, "sought out more supporting than opposing arguments" pertaining to those issues. More striking, well-informed participants were bigger offenders than their less informed counterparts.[3] "Citizens," in sum, "overly accommodate supportive evidence while dismissing out-of-hand evidence that challenges their prior attitudes." That goes "especially" for "the most sophisticated."[4]

Experts, and not only in politics, can be worse in this respect than non-experts. The psychologist Philip Tetlock, in a famous study of economic and political prediction, found that "those who know more forecast very slightly better than those who know less. But those with the most knowledge are often less reliable" because "the person who acquires more knowledge develops an enhanced illusion of her skill." The resulting overconfidence is one reason that experts may prove no better at prediction than "dart throwing monkeys."[5] A lot of knowledge is a dangerous thing.

Here, then, is one reason for educators to aim at the reasonable person, who thinks nothing more unworthy of a rational being than refusing to yield to the better argument. Those who adopt this aim confront directly a problem as observable in Locke's seventeenth century as it is in our twenty-first. Even a person in full command of tools to identify and defeat prejudice fixates on "the prejudices that mislead other men or parties, as if he . . . had none of his own." Almost no one "is ever brought fairly to examine his own principles." By principles, Locke means general rules, whether they concern morality or not, that guide our thoughts and actions. One needn't be a pessimist to think that people little disposed to question "prejudices imbibed from education, party, reverence, fashion [and] interest," though they may appear to be competent, are protected only by luck from making dangerous mistakes.[6]

They're also not free. The person who cannot be "brought fairly to examine his own principles," derived from miscellaneous sources neither willed nor understood by him, doesn't think for himself.

Yes, I know that there are limits to our intellectual freedom. Tocqueville explains that a "man who would undertake to examine everything by himself . . . would keep his mind in a perpetual agitation." We live by too many rules to examine them all for ourselves. I ask my political philosophy students why I shouldn't, supposing I'm sure I won't get caught, murder someone for money. If I had to rely on their ability to back up their strong prejudice against hitmen, I would have murdered someone for money long ago. Yet it's good for them and for their country, which frowns on murder for hire, that they often rely on what they've been taught about morality, instead of withholding assent until they've acquired enough philosophy to nail things down. Although Tocqueville concedes that "every man who receives an opinion on the word of another puts his mind in slavery," he calls it "a salutary servitude" without which people would not be able to use the freedom they have.[7]

We can accept this humbling proposition, however, and still honor the spirit of Tocqueville's *Democracy in America*, which addresses itself to those "who see in the freedom of the intellect something holy." Tocqueville thought that the unchecked authority of the majority "might in the end confine the action of

individual reason within narrower limits than befit the greatness and happiness of the human species."[8] When he reminds
his readers that we always "encounter authority somewhere in
the intellectual and moral world," Tocqueville isn't urging sur-
render. Rather, he's warning us that the independence from
individual tyrants of which democrats boast masks the tyranny
of the majority.[9] And Tocqueville exhorts us to secure as much
intellectual freedom as we can in a time not nearly as hospitable
to it as we think. That's why Allan Bloom could say, "Tocqueville
taught me the importance of the university to democratic society," which consists especially in "preserving the freedom of
the mind."[10]

We don't create ourselves or even construct our beliefs about
the world without borrowed premises. But within those limits,
liberal education, an education in freedom, shapes people who
hold up their opinions—about raising children, or caring for
friends, or practicing politics—to rational scrutiny.

I concede that colleges and universities should also train
people to deal with complex ideas and situations. We need
people conversant with complexity to run our hospitals, plan
our retirements, and defend our shores. But reasonable people
have that covered. People who think it disgraceful not to yield
to the better argument resist simplifying distortions. The re-
verse isn't true. A person can delight in dealing with complexity
without having the least interest in examining his own principles. And people who don't have the least interest in examining
their own principles are trouble.

Almost no one "is ever brought fairly to examine his own
principles." As mindful as we are that smart people do stupid
things, we have nothing on Locke when it comes to identifying
the failure of what passes for education. Even "men of study and
thought" who "reason right" and are "lovers of truth," Locke

says, can lack the discipline required to notice that "the grounds upon which we bottom our reasoning" reflect our narrow experience. Most of the people we call learned are like inhabitants of an isolated island who, because they have never encountered a rival, think themselves "the wisest people of the universe." They think they're liberated but talk only to people who share their assumptions. Worse, and probably more common, are those "who put passion in the place of reason" and "neither use their own nor hearken to other people's reason any farther than it suits their humor, interest, or party." They are able "to talk and hear reason" but content themselves with self-righteously spouting self-serving sophisms.[11]

We worry, as if we were in a state of crisis, about correcting particular biases, or about whether our graduates can locate Vietnam on a map, or about how well they score on aptitude tests. But we hardly worry about whether the student who scores an A on an essay is what Locke calls a "logical chicaner"—a person merely skilled in debate—or a "man of reason," who seeks to improve his understanding. These are "the two most different things" Locke knows of, but the education he criticizes fails to produce one more reliably than another.[12] As for us, the distinction is barely on our educational radar. Even the people who succeed in college by the various metrics we use to gauge success may be fools. Now that's a crisis, made no less alarming by the inability of any civilization we know of to resolve it satisfactorily.

Constructive Shaming

One way of explaining how politics makes us stupid is that, in politics, we often become shameless, or at least ashamed of the wrong things. We bend all our efforts toward winning a political argument, even when those efforts cause us perversely to assert untrue or grossly exaggerated things. When that happens, something has overcome in us the widely shared opinion that it debases a person to stray so far from good sense. Perhaps we just want to have our own way and don't mind dirtying ourselves to have it. If we do feel shame, it's only at being the kind of loser who isn't clever or tough enough to exploit others. Or it may be, instead, that one is passionately committed to a partisan cause. In that case, acknowledging even a kernel of truth in the other side's position, or calling out one's own side for making hyperbolic claims, seems squishy. We're much more ashamed of that squishiness than of going further than the evidence permits, so we suppress our doubts. The tendency to cling to a view after one can no longer offer serious arguments in its defense, though especially notable in politics, is present in every area in which our passions or interests are engaged, from religion to morality to child care to business strategy.

Another reason for liberal education to aim at the reasonable person, then, is that such a person is ashamed of the right things. Remember that we're willing to call someone who honors reason a reasonable person, even if she is so far merely an apprentice. When that person says that nothing misbecomes a rational being more than persisting in a plainly irrational argument, she means that one ought to be ashamed of such persistence. Contemporary critics of Locke sometimes complain of his use of shame in education, and Locke does call "esteem and disgrace" the "most powerful incentives to the mind."[13] But in light of the daunting obstacles to our attempts to be reasonable and the prodigious power of shame, which persists despite our aversion to many forms of shaming, it would be foolish not to try to make use of it.

Mark Edmundson, a professor of English at the University of Virginia who has written extensively on humanities education, tells of a Columbia University instructor who, legend has it, asked his students, "One: what book did you most dislike in the course? Two: What intellectual or characterological flaws in you does that dislike point to?"[14] Edmundson admits that the question is heavy-handed but approves the idea behind it. Students should come to see education as a test not mainly of their capacity to perform on exam day but of their capacity to become a worthy audience for works of great merit. If they find Shakespeare a bore, is it possible that they, not Shakespeare, have failed to rise to the occasion? Edmundson opens his essay with a description of course evaluation day in his classroom, when his students, who usually need a zany anecdote to get going, toil away with great attention and energy. The course has to make itself worthy of them, not the other way around. If Edmundson has been on his game, students will bestow on him the highest honor, that they found his class "enjoyable." My own, too kind, students can live with even less than enjoyment, giving high scores so long as class isn't grating: "I didn't even mind going!"

College education should, as we now like to say, spark joy, and teachers have to meet students where they are. But since we regularly fail to follow arguments where they lead, fail to persist in thinking when thinking gets hard, and fail to stick with arguments that threaten our self-confidence, good teachers have to make us feel these vices. A course that we merely enjoy can't do that. Joseph Cropsey, my first political philosophy professor, would sometimes say "Courage!" when we came upon an especially difficult passage. But any work that requires courage puts us at risk of displaying cowardice. We shouldn't whip ourselves too hard over a common and understandable failing, but we couldn't honor reason if we didn't also think it dishonorable to run away from it.

Reminds me of Bartalou

If one feels corny about imitating Cropsey, it's not because shame is passé. Rather, as Edmundson argues, the standards of praise and blame that govern student life are poorly aligned with the standards of praise and blame that suit a community of learners. While Edmundson depicts his students as more passionless than irrational, he sees them as anything but shameless. Rather, they're tyrannized by the reigning opinion that one shouldn't take education, except as a vehicle for success, too seriously. "You're inhibited, except on ordained occasions, from showing emotion, stifled from trying to achieve anything original. You're made to feel that even the slightest departure from the reigning code will get you genially ostracized. This is a culture tensely committed to a laid-back norm."[15] One doesn't have to agree with Edmundson that consumerism is to blame for this state of affairs to think his description at least partly right. If one doesn't find a way to begin to substitute new standards of praise and blame for the reigning ones, learning will be, apart from the rare student who bucks the norms, superficial.

Edmundson's piece is more than two decades old, and his portrayal of students as cool doesn't quite fit the passionate student protesters who have dominated media portrayals of campus life in recent years. But shame is no less powerful a force for student activists than it is for those who find caring uncool. The activists and those influenced by them, according to Jonathan Haidt and Greg Lukianoff, inhabit a "call-out culture," which rewards "people who shame or punish alleged offenders" against social justice.[16] Think of the incident at Yale I referred to in chapter 2. Nicholas Christakis, whose designation as professor of social and natural sciences suggests a man prepared for many contingencies, could do little to appease his students, one of whom, with that combination of vulgarity ("Who the fuck hired you?") and moralism now in fashion, told him that he was "disgusting" and "should not sleep at night." In short, Christakis should have been ashamed of himself.

Of what, exactly? Christakis's spouse, Erika Christakis, an expert on child development, had written an email questioning Yale's approach to offensive Halloween costumes. That approach consisted mainly of counseling students to err on the side of inoffensiveness. Erika observed that what counted as offensive was open to dispute. She added, now speaking as a "child development specialist," that Yale's attempt to "control" young people's Halloween choices suggested a dim "view of young adults, of their strength and judgment."[17]

Reasonable people can disagree about whether Yale was offering friendly advice or "control" to its students, but that wasn't the heart of the matter for student critics. Nicholas deserved to be shamed, as they saw it, partly because he seemed to endorse Erika's harmful Halloween heterodoxies, and partly because he thought the matter worth discussing at all. Concerning the latter offense, Nicholas was told that his effort to make "an intellectual space" of the residence hall over which he and Erika presided was not only misplaced but a reason to demand his resignation.[18] Although Nicholas remains a member of the faculty at Yale, both Christakises felt compelled to resign as resident masters, so powerful was the backlash against the attempt to make an argument, grounded in expertise, about a controversial matter.[19]

The love of justice sometimes moves a person to seek out the best evidence and arguments available, and student activists are often thoughtful. However, the call-out culture is no friendlier to education than Edmundson's culture of cool, with which it coexists.[20] What's lacking, for the most part, outside of some individual classrooms, is a standard of praise and blame according to which it's shameful to close one's mind.

Objections and Replies

A sensible person might now interject that there are many, more pressing, things to be ashamed of than being unreasonable, such as abandoning a friend when the going is hard, or selling out one's country. I'll have something to say about that when I take up the relationship between liberal and civic education later in this chapter. I'll say now, following Locke's lead, that becoming a reasonable person is the crown, not the whole, of an education.

Take, for example, cowardice, which seems on its face to be more shameful than being stubbornly unreasonable. "Without courage," Locke grants, "a man will scarce keep steady to his duty and fill the character of a truly worthy man." Locke, therefore, recommends working on a child's courage from very early on, and delivering him to higher education with a mind that has "mastery over itself and its usual fears."[21] Whatever the defects of early education today—some worry that children are raised to fear too many things—we, too, can expect that young people arrive at college with at least minimal character training. Though such training might fail, efforts will have been made to render young people disinclined to run away from a fly, to sell out a friend for money, or to neglect their studies for food, drink, and sex. They will have begun to receive this training before reason is much developed in them. Becoming a reasonable person doesn't crowd out the aim of becoming a courageous, just, or moderate person.

However, Locke is after the courage "of a rational creature." English education, Locke acknowledges, succeeds in shaping adults willing to "venture their lives for their country," who show "courage in the field" and fearlessness "in the face of an enemy." Yet it fails reliably to shape people for what Locke calls

"true fortitude," the "quiet possession of a man's self and an un-
disturbed doing his duty, whatever evil besets or danger lies in
his way."[22] First, it neglects the uses of fear, which was "given us
as a monitor to quicken our industry and keep us upon our
guard against the approaches of evil." A fearless person would
soon be dead. The "resolution of a rational creature" differs
from the "brutish fury" of the berserker who charges into danger without consideration of the usefulness or likely consequences of his action. Second, the English education in courage
neglects dangers that "attack us in other places besides the fields
of battle." Though "death be the king of terrors, yet pain, disgrace, and poverty have frightful looks" that "discompose most
men." The same person who has been trained to be perfectly
calm in the presence of a lion may lose her composure when
people ridicule her, even if the people ridiculing her are poor
judges. Such a person, though useful in some situations, particularly those involving large feline predators, will, on the
whole, be of little use to herself or others. What's wanted is a
courage consistent with a "just estimate of the danger,"[23] a courage that lets in enough fear to "keep us awake and excite our
attention, industry, and vigor" but does "not disturb the calm
use of our reason" or "hinder the execution of what that
dictates."[24]

It's a standing, gentle, joke among my colleagues that no
matter what the literary or philosophical text, our students dis-
till it into some version of "stand up for what you believe in."
Our task is not to disabuse them of this worthy sensibility; most
of us are ourselves no fans of the unprincipled or cowardly. Instead, with the aid of our texts and their different understandings of what one should believe in, and of the obstacles to putting principle into practice, we ask our students to step back and
consider whether what they want is good and what standing up

for it might entail. While these are philosophical questions, they're also questions that impose themselves on people who hope to help their friends, or their families, or their country, rather than inadvertently to harm them.

Even after we adopt a standard of praise and blame according to which it's disgraceful not to listen to reason, things that were disgraceful before, like cowardice, don't stop being disgraceful. But the reasonable person is the sort who considers, as Locke does, the possibility that much of what passes for courage is narrow and foolish. And at least some of the reasonable person's courage will be displayed in her willingness, if necessary, to be designated a coward by people of narrow and defective understandings. The reasonable person, to repeat, is ashamed of the right things.

But that way of putting it provokes another objection. Conservatives have been known to accuse left-wing professors of indoctrinating their students. Yet I've endorsed the idea that professors should try to shape their students, in part by influencing their understanding of what's shameful. That raises the suspicion, one felt by some of Locke's readers, that when students accept the authority of reason, they're really accepting the authority of teachers, who have stacked the deck in favor of a way of life they or those who pay the bills find congenial. Rather than being liberated or bettered, such students have traded one form of mental unfreedom for another, a "new mode of domination and subjection."[25]

The use of shame alone needn't worry us much. We've already noticed that reason's strength shouldn't be overestimated. About a closely related matter, Locke's use of custom in education, the political philosopher and Locke scholar Ruth Grant, says, "Custom is powerful but not authoritative. Reason is authoritative but largely ineffectual. . . . The only solution is to enlist custom's power in the service of reason's authority."[26] The same can be said of shame, which here is used to support, when it might otherwise undermine, our examination of our own principles. The difference between an education that uses shame to encourage submission to a tyrant's capricious will and one that uses it to encourage submission to the best available arguments doesn't dissolve because both educations make use of shame.

However, Grant concedes some ground to the objection we're considering, which not only worries about the use of shame but also suggests that what poses as reasonableness is prejudice. "Even the Lockean principle that reason is authoritative, but custom is not," for example, "should be subjected to critical examination." Perhaps it won't be if colleges and universities shape students whose custom is to scrutinize customs. Conservatives who praise custom as a repository of wisdom will be with Grant when she warns that "a 'culture of reasonableness' can become a new orthodoxy."[27]

This is a genuine danger, particularly because a community devoted to becoming reasonable can't pretend to be neutral about the goodness of that aim. Locke himself is mindful that teaching, too often, "when looked into, amounts to no more but making [students] imbibe their teachers' notions and tenets." But the teachers who receive Locke's praise "freely expose their principles to the test" and "are pleased to have them examined" so that "they themselves, as well as others, may not lay any stress upon any received proposition beyond what the evidence of its truth will warrant."[28] Their injunction to be reasonable, unlike the injunction to submit one's will to a tyrant, invites investigation and challenge. Any teaching can harden into orthodoxy, but the general spirit of liberal education is inhospitable to orthodoxies, even when they're advanced by the militantly unorthodox.

Can Colleges Shape Their Students?

Perhaps some readers are now convinced that shaping reasonable people is desirable since only such people are free and because merely smart and learned people are often fools. Perhaps some of those readers are also convinced that to shape reasonable people one needs somehow to win them over to new standards of praise and blame. So maybe that would all be great. But is it possible?

Anyone who has spent time in a classroom might doubt the power of colleges and universities to influence the standards of praise and blame that guide their students. It's all we can do, after all, to get students to stop deleting our emails. Yet we also know that students in large numbers can be initiated into communities whose standards are quite different from the ones they walked in with.

In a scientific community, for example, members, however competitive and ambitious they may be, are expected to channel their ambition into the pursuit of a common good, the truth about nature, or at least the best working model of it they can develop. To achieve this aim, they share their findings, often across the national and other boundaries that otherwise divide people, and submit them to the scientific community to be confirmed or debunked. They become proud of pursuing the truth via experiment, and therefore of their readiness to live with the ground shifting underneath their feet. John Dewey, the twentieth-century philosopher from whom I borrow this description of the scientific community, may have been wrong to offer it as the model for all communities of reasoners, and to welcome the "general adoption of the scientific attitude in human affairs."[29] But I suspect he's right that new members of a scientific community adopt new standards of praise and blame that often bleed from the classroom and the lab into the way they see themselves altogether. That's how it looks to me when I teach advanced science students.

Similarly, professionals, like the journalist, the doctor, and even the much-maligned lawyer, don't just work a job. Each profession has standards, intellectual and moral, that, whether they're always honored or not, define praiseworthy and shameful activity. This is the kind of work people consider a vocation, work experienced as a call that makes demands on and reshapes a person. One isn't, as a rule, initiated into such vocations as an undergraduate, and not always in schools at all. But the success, however incomplete, of such professions at transmitting their standards to new recruits should make us optimistic about initiating students into a new kind of community, a community of reasonable people. We needn't settle for satisfying our customers, as if their standards of praise and blame were forever fixed.

I admit that being a lawyer or scientist is a more concrete and obviously attractive goal than being a reasonable person. If you ask entering students what they hope to get out of college, I doubt even one will say, "I hope to become reasonable." Yet colleges have long aspired to transform their students, not simply into members of a profession or discipline, but into human beings with virtues that those students probably didn't enter college to acquire. Even today, Andrew Delbanco argues in *College: What It Was, Is, and Should Be*, the American college retains some of the spirit of pre–Civil War, religiously affiliated, colleges. Such colleges, "whatever their particular creed in what has been aptly called 'an age of moral pedagogy' . . . agreed that their primary purpose remained the development of sound character in their students."[30]

This purpose persists even in research universities, although they're more apt to justify themselves in terms of the production of new knowledge. Dewey, a champion of such universities, argued that education was needed precisely to change the mental dispositions of students, whose parents were still stuck in ways of thinking ill-suited for a democratic future. That future depended on "a change in the quality of mental disposition—an educative change." To develop the qualities of mind and character appropriate for emerging democratic conditions, one had to "produce in schools a projection . . . of the society we should like to realize and [form] minds in accord with it."[31] Although Dewey here speaks of education in general, he expects higher education to assist in the "enormous task of liberating the American public mind."[32]

The University of Chicago's Robert Maynard Hutchins, among the most influential college presidents in American history, was a Dewey critic and an advocate for a general education centered on the great books of Western civilization. But his ambition to transform students was hardly, if at all, less than Dewey's. Hutchins spoke of the purpose of the university as "the single-minded pursuit of the intellectual virtues." That pursuit, however, leading us into our intellectual inheritance, gives the university an additional aim, which Hutchins also described as the purpose of education, "to connect man with man, to connect the present with the past, and to advance the thinking of the race." Like Dewey, Hutchins expects that the university, by transforming students, will transform civilization, which may, as a result, "outgrow the love of money."[33]

My point isn't that either Dewey or Hutchins is right but rather that both, though associated with the new research universities, share with the old colleges the ambition to transform individuals not obviously seeking transformation. Each puts himself at the head of, in Hutchins's words, an "evangelistic movement"[34] toward a kind of education that, though not quite in tune with the times, and consequently, not quite in tune with what students and parents want, can succeed. Dewey and Hutchins may not have changed the course of civilization, but they were immensely influential and have shaped the souls of countless students.

It's ambitious to think that higher education can shape students, who often come to college seeking very different things than we want to give them. But that ambition is fully in keeping with the tradition of American higher education. Today, we should be more surprised by its absence than its presence.

"U" Is for Useful: Appealing to Mixed Motives

Compared to these evangelists, we have an easier sell. Locke, for example, at least begins with eminently practical considerations. Although Locke addresses himself mainly to people he calls gentlemen, who have time for study, a gentleman is a "man of business," adept at managing his estate. He is also a man of affairs, capable of being "useful in his country" by, for example, playing a role in the justice system.[35] The gentleman is no egghead. He may cultivate his reasoning and widen his experience by reading ancient authors, but he finds those ancient authors valuable because they "observed and painted mankind well and give the best light into that kind of knowledge."[36] One can hardly deny that a man of business or affairs needs to know what good teachers can teach about the ways of other people.

Locke admits that much of what teachers traditionally push on students, including musty books, is a "deal of trash," useless and never to be thought of again.[37] But the taming of the mind and widening of experience that Locke recommends includes subjects like ethics, history, and poetry. A "comprehensive enlargement of mind . . . assisted with letters, and a free consideration of the several views and sentiments of thinking men of all sides" suits "a soul devoted to truth." But it isn't impractical or, as we say with a hint of contempt, "academic."[38] Rather, everyone should pursue such an enlargement of mind to the extent opportunity affords because the understanding is the "last resort a man has recourse to in the conduct of himself" in every important matter.[39]

This approach to education, though it comes to us courtesy of an Englishman, has deep roots in American thought. Benjamin Franklin, his *Autobiography* explains, formed a "club of mutual improvement" called "the Junto." The club sounds like a philosophy seminar, in which each member is required to produce "one or more queries on any point of Morals, Politics, or Natural Philosophy, to be discussed by the company," and also to write, once every three months, an essay on a subject of his choice. Debates, in the spirit of Locke, were "to be conducted in the sincere spirit of inquiry after truth, without fondness for dispute." Yet club members, many of them clerks or tradesmen, apparently saw no conflict between the kind of work they were doing in the Junto and their desire for professional advancement, nor did they have any difficulty moving from philosophical queries to plans for a neighborhood watch.[40] No doubt, members of the Junto, and the larger group of people Franklin calls "lovers of reading,"[41] take pleasure in self-improvement, rather than regarding it as an unpleasant means to a desirable end. At the same time, Franklin's pursuit of the truth in the company of others, and with the help of books, is never disentangled from Franklin's practical aims. The *Autobiography* is a classic rags-to-riches story and Franklin, like Locke, has enough regard for what motivates his readers to propose that he who chooses to love reason may just get rich.

Because of this, I get less annoyed than some devotees of liberal education when colleges try to sell their usefulness.[42] The literary theorist and all-around curmudgeon, Stanley Fish, isn't alone in insisting that the humanities, at least, are quite useless.[43] Suppose we agree with Fish, for argument's sake, that the purpose of the university is contemplation rather than practice, or with his inspiration, the philosopher Michael Oakeshott, that we want an undergraduate to come to college "to seek his intellectual fortune."[44] Suppose, too, we agree that when universities justify themselves in practical terms, they risk being judged solely on that basis. These agreements shouldn't stop us from acknowledging that even people who may come to take great delight in what goes on at the university, and to value the pursuit of truth for its own sake, enter with, and even graduate with, mixed motives. Plato has never been rivaled in his portrait of the pleasures of friendship founded on the pursuit of the truth. But even he wasn't above, in his account of Socrates, suggesting that teachers of reason benefit polities and individuals who may never come to value philosophy for its own sake.[45]

We should be clear with ourselves and with our students that becoming reasonable people is not the equivalent of learning how to win friends and influence people. We should even be wary, as we'll see when we consider liberal education and civic education, of suggesting that becoming reasonable is the equivalent of eating one's vegetables or performing community service. But we shouldn't turn our noses up at the kind of practical pitch for education that Franklin perfected.

The student drawn in by such a pitch may find that being part of a community of reasonable people is worthwhile for other reasons. Consider Earl Shorris, whose project to teach humanities to the poor I introduced in chapter 1. At first, he pitches his course as a way of learning what rich people learn. "You've been cheated," he says. The rich, because they learn to reflect on things instead of reacting impulsively, figure out "how to use politics to get along, to get power." Shorris also appeals to pride. "I think you're the elites," he tells his prospective students. When the course starts, Shorris explains that he will be less a lecturer than a midwife, helping students give birth to the knowledge they possess in embryo. One of his students later reflects that "it was the first time anyone had ever paid attention to their opinions." This is still a kind of pride, but the kind that measures worth in terms of one's membership in a community of reasoners and potential knowers. During the course, one of Shorris's students phones him about a problem he had been dealing with at work. Shorris fears the worst, but the student has called because he is proud that, in a situation in which he might once have reacted impulsively, he stepped back and asked himself, "What would Socrates do?"[46] Like the young person who asks, "What would Jesus do?," this young person has been drawn into a new community with new standards.

Part of Shorris's success resembles that of a good coach. He sets high expectations, instills pride in students, and shows that he cares about and is willing to work for their success. He makes his students feel that they are engaged, with him, in important work. The comparison of teacher to coach can be dispiriting. Imagine a basketball coach presented with a group of players who aren't sure they're interested in the game and are perhaps not even aware that they're expected to play basketball. Liberal educators can expect to feel like that coach frequently. The skeptic with whom I opened this section, who wonders how teachers can influence their students at all, is no fool. Still, at least one award-winning professor, Joe Hoyle, tells us that he looks to the legendary coach, Vince Lombardi, for inspiration, particularly to one quotation. "A man," Lombardi says, "can be as great as he wants to be. If you believe in yourself and have the courage, the determination, the dedication, the competitive drive and if you are willing to sacrifice the little things in life and pay the price for the things that are worthwhile, it can be done."[47]

Hoyle teaches accounting.

Not every teacher has to channel Vince Lombardi. That's not my style. But teachers, who now have thrust into their inboxes the latest studies of the latest techniques grounded in the latest in cognitive psychology, shouldn't underestimate the good, old-fashioned, power of the student-teacher relationship. Nor should they underestimate the appeal, which Franklin understood well, of a community of reasoners, participation in which may be even more appealing than participation in a community of accountants. Most teachers have felt, as students, the excitement of not relying on authority in the most important matters, of making progress in their understanding of those matters, and of making that progress in the company of others, whose achievements don't subtract from but rather add to one's own. Our students can, too. Once, one of mine chided me for merely listening to everyone's answers and commenting on them. He wanted me to ask more questions, to probe his answers, to put him to the test. He had learned from other teachers, as Shorris's students did, the appeal of being taken seriously, which did not mean being patted on the head, or even having one's view considered. Being taken seriously meant, for this student, recognizing that he wouldn't be satisfied with less than an answer that could hold up under scrutiny. It meant treating him as the kind of person who would be ashamed to settle for a merely plausible answer when a better one might be available. It meant treating him as a reasonable person.

He was, I hasten to add, atypical. But a teacher, particularly one living in a democratic country, can't assume that only a few elite students can be shaped along those lines, or that only teachers and a handful of students are reasonable people. My mother, who, grew up relatively poor and dropped out of Brooklyn College, was interested enough in the one philosophy class she took to keep some of the books and to encourage her children to take an interest in them. After she died, I found that she had kept almost nothing behind as a record of what she thought, apart from a paper she wrote for that class, in which she was asked to make a case for the kind of life she intended to lead. The teacher who devised that assignment took the risk of expecting his students to reflect on serious and difficult matters, an expectation one fears one might not be able to help one's students to meet. But it insults our students to imagine there's nothing in them that responds to that kind of summons.

As Mr. Cropsey would say, "Courage."

Books and Longings

Locke is not my man in every respect. For one thing, as I indicated in chapter 1, liberal education as I understand it involves the study of old books. Locke recommends old books, including ancient ones. But such books aren't central to his plan. In some ways, the thrust of his argument makes us skeptical that books are "profitable employments of our time" and suspicious that "bookish men" fail to attain "solid and true knowledge."

Locke counsels readers not to accept on authority what can be confirmed only by one's own mind. The reader influenced by Locke searches in books for "proofs," which she then examines for "truth or falsehood," "probability or improbability." Consequently, Lockean readers might not give themselves up to a book, even for a time, preferring instead to "see and follow the train" of an author's "reasonings, observe the strength and clearness of their connection, and examine upon what they bottom." Although Locke recognizes that different kinds of matters need different kinds of proof, he has his readers approach books like a mathematician looking at the works of older mathematicians for tips.[48]

There are two problems with this sensible-sounding approach. The first is the presumption that you can learn much from a carefully constructed book by reducing it to the terms of a logical proof. The second is the presumption that the student already has the tools to judge works that generations have handed down to her with a recommendation to profit from them. When we look at books recommended to us in this way, as collections of observations and reasonings auditioning for acceptance on our terms, we, like Edmundson's students, discount the possibility that we should accept the author's terms instead.

Locke's advice is mostly sound. An author, old or new, is finally to be judged by the "evidence he produces and the conviction he affords us, drawn from things themselves."[49] But the "Show me!" attitude of the man from Missouri or of the impatient venture capitalist who won't buy anything you can't sell her in ten minutes is ill-suited to learning what one doesn't already know. Locke, although he advocates careful reading and prods us to view familiar standards skeptically, can put us in that frame of mind about books.

Yet Locke also explains why a community of reasoners needs old books. No one is free, he says, even the sincerest follower of reason, from narrowness. We "see but in part, and we know but in part, and therefore it is no wonder we conclude not right from our partial views." To a point, this natural defect can be remedied by conversing with others. Locke recommends that one converse even with those who "come short of him in capacity, quickness, and penetration."[50] Their experience might widen ours. But even if we expand our circle to include contemporaries from other cultures, it's safe to assume that our time, like all times we know of, has shared prejudices. At Ursinus College, our first-year seminar begins with Plato's image of human beings as prisoners chained up in a cave. Even those who appear most cosmopolitan and conversant in the ideas of their time and place are imprisoned by those same ideas, to which they can't imagine alternatives. Many worthy answers to our most important questions will, as Allan Bloom says, "go against the grain of . . . our times," so that "book learning," though far from the "whole of education," is "necessary."[51] That's one reason why Locke, who makes fun of those who "will not admit an opinion not authorized by men of old, who were then all giants of knowledge," also criticizes excessive fondness for "modern inventions and discoveries."[52]

If Locke makes reverence for ancient books more of a target than disregard for them, it's likely because his seventeenth-century reader still needs to be told to "use his eyes." The great astronomer and physicist, Galileo, skewered people who "put the testimony of writers ahead of what experience shows" them, the kind who reject unrefuted reasons and solid evidence merely because they contradict Aristotle.[53] Although the scientific revolution had made some headway by the time Locke was writing, excessive reverence for the ancients and pride in one's

capacity to cite ancient works still needed combatting, particularly in the realm of education. Reverence is, to say the least, not
our problem. We, full of unearned irreverence, taught to "doubt
beliefs even before [we] believed in anything," are more likely
to imagine that we have nothing to learn from the ancients
than we are to overestimate them.[54] We are entirely too confident that we can see with our own eyes and unaware of the
narrowness of our field of vision. For us, old books are nearly
essential.

There is one other way in which Locke is not my man. To
explain it, I need to bring up his rival in education and politics,
Jean-Jacques Rousseau. Rousseau and Locke are known mainly
by their differences. Locke was among the fathers of the political liberalism fought for by American revolutionaries and en-
shrined in the Declaration of Independence. Rousseau criticized that liberalism and influenced the French Revolution,
which outstripped America's in radicalism. Locke wrote the
most influential educational work of the seventeenth century,
Some Thoughts Concerning Education. Rousseau's eighteenth-
century educational novel, *Emile*, took Locke on directly and
largely succeeded in spoiling Locke's reputation as an educational theorist. Yet, in spite of these differences, Locke and
Rousseau aimed at nearly the same thing. The person who
emerges from Rousseau's education, just like the person who
emerges from Locke's, should permit, as much as possible, "no
other authority [to] govern him beyond that of his own
reason."[55]

Rousseau introduces this standard amid a discussion of an
overwhelming challenge to rationality, namely, adolescence.
Rousseau's young protagonist, Emile, is on fire, full of longing
for a still indeterminate object, specifically for a girl, but generally for connection with something beyond the self. You can

read Locke's educational works a hundred times and never notice that he says nearly nothing about this phenomenon. But as soon as you've read *Emile*, an educational work that takes educating adolescent desire seriously, you become aware of something missing, not only from Locke but also from our own educational ideas. Those ideas are long on sex education but short on how to educate the kind of creature who falls in love.

This is no place to discuss the details of *Emile*, which includes—spoiler alert—a carefully orchestrated courtship and marriage. Suffice it to say that Emile reads works like Plato's dialogue on love, the *Symposium*. He doesn't read them primarily for good information about other human beings, though his prior education has prepared him to seek and make use of such information. Nor does he read them to boil them down to their simplest logical components. He reads them to "feel and to love the beautiful of all sorts."[56] This aspect of Rousseau's *Emile* doesn't mean that Rousseau has abandoned the aim of educating reasonable people. It means that a reasonable approach to education can't discount the power of a student's longings, which, it turns out, aren't wholly for self-improvement. Nor can it discount the importance to a person's happiness of how he makes sense of and pursues those longings.

I've already said that I don't get annoyed when students sell their usefulness. But even as we sweat profusely over the long-term future of liberal education, we shouldn't give up the claim that we have more to offer youthful longing than a broad-minded attitude toward booze and sex.

I'll have more to say about colleges in the next chapter. But now is a good time to observe that the students I know, though pragmatists in some respects—many worry about what job their majors might lead to—are romantics in others. Many come to college expecting to be changed in an ill-defined but big way. The hard work, then, is not convincing students that there's more to life than "making it." If we shouldn't be shy about selling the leg up our students will have in the world of work, we shouldn't be shy about defending colleges and universities as more than career development offices with classrooms attached. The hard work is making those classrooms, and other parts of campus, believable as places in which one might become reasonable.

The Need for Judgment

Perhaps the biggest obstacle to making classrooms and other parts of campus believable as places in which one might become reasonable is that few have confidence in reason. Granted, most students and non-students have confidence in it when it takes on its properly godlike mathematical or scientific form. Even doubters of evolution rarely doubt the whole scientific enterprise. And although some intellectuals say that science is merely an interpretation of the world, as culture-bound as other such interpretations, we're grateful that science has granted us high-fidelity headphones to tune them out. In mathematical and scientific reason, most of my students believe with almost perfect faith. But it's hard for us to conceive of a kind of reason that isn't mathematical or scientific.

To understand why that may be hard, take my own field of political science. I'll treat this example at some length, so let me preface the treatment with an explanation of its significance. The study of politics, I claim (following others), is like the study of a wide range of phenomena that have this in common: they all demand that we make our way toward the truth without the formulas and methods that help us find our way when we're looking strictly at relationships of cause and effect. They all demand judgment.

Despite the "science" in its name, political science includes people like me, who study old books, and who might feel at home in a department of philosophy. My relationship with colleagues is peculiar. Suppose I ask my hallmate, "What have you been up to?" She might reply, "I'm trying to figure out whether allowing people to register to vote prior to the age of eighteen—a policy called preregistration—increases youth turnout. I'm looking at data available in the Current Population Survey and comparing turnout in states that have preregistration to states that don't. If I use sound statistical methods to control for other variables, I should be able to determine whether preregistration is an effective policy or not." I might congratulate her on pursuing an empirical question resolvable in principle by weighing and measuring. Now suppose, to be polite, she asks me what I'm doing. I might answer, "Reading Rousseau's *Emile*. Again. To deepen my understanding of how to educate free people." She might nod politely, but the thought bubble above her head will read, "Freak."

My colleague, whether her study succeeds or not, strives to be scientific. If all goes well, her weighing and measuring will put her on more solid ground than previous students of voting behavior occupied, so that she and her colleagues can be confident they're making progress. They won't need to go back to eighteenth-century texts to advance their understanding of politics, since eighteenth-century thinkers, in their access to data and their ability to use statistical methods to interpret it, were like children compared to a well-trained twenty-first-century political scientist. In contrast, in political philosophy, one learns not only from eighteenth-century thinkers but also from old interpretations of such thinkers. The latest paper on Plato in the *American Political Science Review* isn't necessarily more helpful than one published in 1950. That suggests—and this is what must seem most bizarre to others in the field of political science—that there's no progress in the study of political philosophy. Why not, then, just kick us political philosophers out?

The short answer is that although it's hard to grasp how reason might work outside of science and mathematics, it's impossible to imagine understanding politics otherwise.

Much of politics can't be understood in scientific terms. Ruth Grant, to whom I'm indebted for the main arguments I make in this section and the next, agrees with her science-minded colleagues that politics involves the kinds of cause and effect relationships that scientists study. Are economically interdependent countries more or less likely to make war on each other? That's a question that, if we define "economic interdependence" and "war" with sufficient precision, may lend itself to scientific study. In some ways, "trying to explain political events is like trying to explain the flow of a river or a cycle of hurricanes."[57] But politics is also "an expression of human purposes and intentions," about whose meaning reasonable people will disagree.[58] "How should we understand the present administration?" is a question that can be approached in part by looking at cause and effect relationships (has the tax policy resulted in higher wages?). But it can't be adequately treated without careful consideration of the players involved, their relationships, and what their words and actions mean. So, trying to explain political events is also "like trying to explain the performance of a symphony or any other conscious collective human activity."[59]

In thinking about politics, then, weighing and measuring gets us somewhere, but the tools of the historian, the journalist, and the critic, are indispensable. So also are the tools of the political philosopher, who "returns to old material in response to new circumstances when those circumstances cannot be adequately understood within the dominant conceptual regime."[60] For example, when we use "demagogue" to describe a politician, we use a term that has a contemporary dictionary definition, to be sure, but also a rich history of reflection on its meaning with which we've largely lost touch. To understand what's going on, to understand whether "demagogue" has a meaning we can use to identify a real problem or is just an insult we hurl at popular politicians we dislike, we probably need to immerse ourselves in that history.

Definitive scientific knowledge of politics eludes us because of the uniqueness and complexity of any political moment. Whether we should reject a war because it's potentially "another Vietnam" depends on difficult and non-scientific estimates of the causes and character of the Vietnam War.[61] Such estimates have something to do with the motives of players at the time, of what their real options were, and even of counterfactual history, what might have happened if different decisions were made. We also need to grasp the motives and options of players now and to try to predict how different policies under consideration might change them. About these things, even after extensive analysis, reasonable people will disagree.

Definitive scientific knowledge of politics eludes us, also, because conscious activity makes politics happen. The precise reason for any given action may be hidden from the actors themselves. About the motive and meaning of a political speech or deed, even astute, careful, coolheaded, nonpartisan students of politics, prepared to follow arguments where they lead, will disagree.

And definitive scientific knowledge of politics eludes us because moral questions matter in politics, and disagreement among reasonable people about the rightness or wrongness of an action can persist forever.

In trying to understand politics, we learn that "the world always remains opaque to us in important respects."[62] For this reason, the study and practice of politics call for judgment, "that faculty at work in any situation where reasonable people might disagree," the kind of situation that can't be dealt with by applying a mathematical formula or conducting a controlled experiment.[63]

From this observation, we might conclude, with thinkers as different as Aristotle and Locke, that different "sorts of things are knowable in different ways and with correspondingly varying degrees of certainty."[64] We might set to work on identifying and teaching the standards and intellectual habits that help us distinguish good from bad arguments when we lack the kinds of arguments that put an end to disagreement. If we can't make meaningful progress in that work, then we're adrift, even if we tend to avoid politics, since so many of our most important decisions—should I intervene to help my friend or leave her alone? Should I put my mother in a home or have her live with me? Should I stay in this job, or risk taking another?—fall between "ignorance and knowledge."[65] We suppose that experience and reflection can help us to become better judges in these matters. We suppose that we can know, and are responsible for trying to know, something about them, that we are not reduced to flipping a coin. But we also know that our defense of a decision, even if it satisfies us, isn't impregnable. The other things we might have decided to do instead won't be ruled out to everybody's satisfaction, in the way that discarded scientific theories have been ruled out.

I began this section by noting the high prestige of the natural sciences and mathematics, and one way of putting our problem is that science and mathematics are the only game in town when it comes to the pursuit of the truth. Our problem isn't that people don't understand that judgment is desperately needed. Whether we define judgment as a single faculty at work in situations in which reasonable people disagree, or as a bundle of skills and virtues that help us negotiate such situations, we can't do without it. It would be hard to find anyone who, when pressed, would deny that. It's therefore distressing that "we seem to have lost our bearings with respect to matters of judgment."[66]

Is Judgment Possible?

No doubt part of the reason we have lost our bearings is the belief, with which Allan Bloom opens *The Closing of the American Mind*, "that truth is relative."[67] But that belief, Bloom acknowledges, doesn't run deep. I'll say more about it in the next chapter. As important, I think, is our skepticism that judgment, however badly we may need it, is possible. Even students, and non-students, who seek firm footing for their beliefs can be brought up short by the suspicion that reasoning isn't reasoning if it can't produce certainty.

It's an exaggeration to say that the natural sciences provide us with certainty or that natural scientists never disagree among themselves. But they do appear to offer a reliable means to put many things, within the limits of the evidence available at any given time, beyond rational dispute. As Francis Bacon, among the most influential theorists of and propagandists for the emerging natural sciences, puts it, even the best minds, without scientific method, "go round for ever in a circle, making trifling, almost contemptible progress."[68] The merely "elegant and probable" ideas of those who, says Bacon in a less charitable mode, may "lack the mental capacity" for experimental science, are smoke compared to the "certain and demonstrable knowledge" that attracts "true sons of learning."[69] There is science, and there is everything else, which is a waste of time.

When, in the seventeenth century, Bacon set out to supplant the frustrating back and forth struggles of philosophers, with a science to put an end to such struggles, it would have been hard to predict his success. Today, if you're not doing science, you may as well be screaming and crying, because there are no standards to settle conflicts between your view and anyone else's.

But there are such standards.

Because the first day of my political philosophy class often coincides with Martin Luther King Day, my students and I read parts of King's "The Power of Nonviolence."[70] Nearly all students come to class disposed in favor of King's argument, whether because King is an icon, or because they dislike violence, or because, on their understanding of the history of the civil rights movement, nonviolent protests work. We begin by looking at some of the premises of King's position, that, for example, behind the "philosophy of nonviolent resistance" is a "philosophy of love." And that behind the improbable idea that love can defeat hate is the belief that "the universe in some form is on the side of justice." "Every person," King says, "who believes in nonviolent resistance" believes that. My students are much less uniformly attracted to that argument. They're at least dimly aware that nonviolence can be a merely strategic maneuver, to be deployed when it's more likely to work than violence, and even as an adjunct to more violent methods. We are, in short, having started with a fuzzy, positive attitude toward nonviolence, now discussing what premises might be underneath a commitment to nonviolence. That "underneath" is at least one of the things we're talking about when we say an argument has depth. And, as everyone knows, deep arguments are usually better than shallow ones.

We also ask what King means by various terms. Some are unfamiliar. What could it mean to be "aggressive spiritually"? Others are familiar but typically unexamined, like "beloved community." In investigating the meanings of those terms as well as we can within the limits of the text we have in front of us and of our own experience, we're trying to get clarity about King's argument. Everyone knows that, other things equal, clear arguments are better than unclear ones.

At some point, a student will point to circumstances under which nonviolence wouldn't have worked. That student is demanding that, rather than generalizing from a single example, we see how our argument for nonviolence fares when we test it against different examples. Everyone knows that comprehensive arguments are better than narrow ones.

Where we cannot gauge our progress mathematically or experimentally, progress can be measured, as Grant thinks progress in political theory can be measured, by "increasing depth, clarity, and comprehensiveness."[71] These aren't the only criteria for distinguishing between strong and weak arguments, but they're among the most common.

When I say that "everyone knows" that some kinds of arguments are better than others, I do so advisedly. As plausible as it may seem when we consider hard science our gold standard, it's implausible, and inconsistent with the standards we adopt when we're not playing at relativism, that "the fact of disagreement" implies "that nothing can be known."[72] Gerald Graff, a professor of English and education, finds continuity between the kinds of everyday arguments, particularly about sports, he engaged in before he became interested in "school," and the arguments in which he wants his students to participate.[73]

No one imagines that people can only scream and cry about whether LeBron James or Michael Jordan is the Greatest of All Time, merely because that question can probably never be settled.[74] There, too, we grasp the difference between deep and shallow, comprehensive and narrow, clear and fuzzy arguments. When we invite students into a community of reasonable people, we're inviting them into a community they have a foot in already.

It's not only so-called relativists, by the way, who have trouble grasping that some things lie in between what we are completely ignorant about and what we can know with certainty. In *God and Man at Yale*, William F. Buckley believes he has caught academics in a contradiction. Either they believe there is a truth, in which case their duty is to transmit it, or they believe there is no truth, in which case they're relativists whose claims to inquire into the truth are ridiculous.[75] Buckley neglects a possibility that a serious person might embrace. There is a truth, but our capacity to grasp it is limited. We tend to think we know the truth when we don't. So we should inquire after it in full awareness of our limits, cautioning ourselves against claiming we know more than we do. This sense that knowledge is elusive, and the caution and humility that should accompany it, is one aspect of the conservatism I outlined in the preface.

The skeptic, the one who points to our difficulty in getting students to stop texting in class, may by now be growing impatient. It's hard even to get students to talk, much less to adopt rigorous argumentative standards. As Graff says, we often "tolerate a low level of articulation and let students vent" instead of "really engaging with—or even listening to—their classmates" because we're happy they're talking at all.[76] But first, students are on to this. "Why should I talk for the sake of talking?" they'll protest during office hours. Silence is at least sometimes the result of the absence, rather than the presence, of standards. Second, the teacher need not deploy these standards to shut students down. I agree with David Hayes's delightful essay, "When BS is a Virtue," that it's important for students to "try to inhabit the author's or artist's point of view, or to try out how certain thoughts feel, or to develop their capacities for belief, sympathetic intelligence, and attachment."[77] Such exploration need not be crushed immediately by demands for evidence, definitions, and responses to counter-examples.

But for the exploration to continue, students need some confidence that it can lead somewhere, that their attachments need not be arbitrary, that they can be reasonable people.

Is Reason Enough? Liberal and Civic Education

Nearly everyone who claims to be doing liberal education also claims to be educating students for citizenship. But if liberal education is about shaping reasonable people, it's not obvious that it's good for citizenship.[78]

In chapter 1, I alluded to the possibility that Socrates, the patron saint of liberal educators, may guide human beings to higher peaks of freedom than Lockean citizens experience. However, that freedom sometimes appears to be freedom from what most of us consider important obligations. Plato depicts a Socrates who avoids public life as much as possible, who neglects the demands of Athens and of his family to pursue a predominantly negative wisdom, the kind that doesn't cure cancer or build buildings. Socrates doesn't inspire his listeners, at least directly, to get involved in politics or pursue social justice. He neither proposes policies nor attends civil rights marches. His "energies," the political theorist Dana Villa tells us, "are devoted to dissolving the crust of convention and the hubristic claim to moral expertise."[79] Whereas Locke's educational works point toward some kind of citizenship, and Locke himself had a public career, Socrates is barely a citizen at all. It doesn't take a diehard conservative to find Socrates's detachment worrying. Socrates's associates include future democrats, but they also include future tyrants and traitors. Perhaps, then, Locke notwithstanding, reasonable people aren't reliable citizens.

Despite this concern, neither liberal democratic leadership nor liberal democratic public opinion, for the most part, presses colleges and universities to teach citizenship directly. Nor have they insisted that colleges and universities teach students to love liberal democracy. We should pause to reflect on this restraint. Thomas Hobbes, author of the influential seventeenth-century work, *Leviathan*, argued that the universities should teach, among other things, "how great a fault it is to speak evil of the sovereign representative."[80] And governments hadn't needed Hobbes to come by the natural enough idea that universities ought to be instruments of their power.[81] Yet in the United States today, although even private universities suck desperately at the government's teat, politicians mostly don't try to meddle in the classroom. Even President Trump's 2019 Executive Order to protect free speech on campus, whatever one thinks of it, purports only to hold universities to standards they, themselves, acknowledge.[82] According to the American Council of Trustees and Alumni, even many state universities refrain from requiring coursework that would give their graduates a "working knowledge of the history, governing documents, and governing institutions of their country."[83] Requiring such coursework would be a far cry from using the universities to prop up the regime. Yet the public doesn't demand even that much.

Perhaps we grasp that if colleges were to proselytize for citizenship, they would become, even more than they are now, partisan battlegrounds. The meaning of citizenship is itself a matter of political dispute, and advocacy for civic education at our colleges and universities, which comes largely from within, is frequently partisan. Some are unsubtly so. In an essay for the *Monkey Cage*, a blog that presents political science research to a wider public, Elizabeth A. Bennion and Melissa R. Michelson explain that Democratic gains in the midterm election depend on student participation. They go on to recommend various means of increasing it, including in-class registration drives. In a subsequent piece, they argue that campus leaders have a civic duty to boost participation and, again, that the classroom is a great place to mobilize young voters. The "actual script is less important than the captive audience."[84] Critics of higher education could not have found better cartoon villains than Professors Bennion and Michelson, who just come out and say that professors should use their classrooms to advance the fortunes of the Democratic Party.

Other calls are subtler but still show how the civic education mission, where it's pursued directly, can conflict with the mission of shaping reasonable people. Martha Nussbaum, at least since *Cultivating Humanity*, has argued that liberal education should aim at "world citizenship." In *Not for Profit*, she ties this aim to another, of winning the society-wide struggle, carried out in each individual soul, between "greed and narcissism" on the one hand, and "respect and love" on the other.[85] Here we have a kind of political religion, whose devotees aspire above all to cosmopolitanism, not patriotism, and pray for love to defeat self-interest. This position is not unreasonable merely because it is a position more likely to be adopted by the center-left than by, say, a libertarian. But there's a tension between adopting, as Nussbaum does, reason as an aim of education and simultaneously adopting a particular, highly contestable, understanding of citizenship as an aim of education. We can imagine the opening speech at orientation, which begins with the exhortation to follow the argument where it leads and ends by telling you exactly where the argument leads—to love. Socrates is a stopover on the flight to John Lennon.

We "all would like to think that wisdom goes our way," Earl Shorris says. Then, not unlike Nussbaum, he proves it by explaining one of the ways he evaluated his course: students had "notably more appreciation for the concepts of benevolence, spirituality, universalism, and collectivism" at the end of it than they did at the beginning. He ends his rich description of his Clemente Course by offering a concrete example of its success, a woman who tries to start a union, not one who joins the Black Panthers or goes to work for her Republican representative.[86] Follow the argument where it leads, says Shorris, but, surprise, it leads to my politics.

That's lucky.

So civic education can find itself at odds with liberal education. Yet, as the political philosopher Martin Diamond has argued, universities do well to offer some kind of civic education. "Someone else always pays" for higher education, and those who give us their money and trust us with their children are entitled to make demands. Where those who pay are governments, and parents and students who accept the legitimacy of those governments, they are entitled to "some form of fidelity to the regime or, at the very least, 'a decent respect to' its fundamental opinions." Both prudence—having no interest in the well-being of one's societal sponsors is a bad look—and principle suggest that colleges and universities should, where they deal with politics, "give to the regime and its opinions a central and respected place."[87] Notice that this concession falls well short of describing the direct aim of higher education as the production of loyal citizens or of adherents to a particular creed.

In the United States, Diamond argues, this concession to the polity does little, if anything, to dilute the aim of shaping reasonable people. For one thing, "a decent stock of received opinions and habits" is probably a more useful starting point for rational inquiry than a vacuum. A student's investment, however unconscious, in the reigning opinions gives her a stake in inquiring into their foundations.[88] When, in my course in American Political Thought, students become interested in the tension between the principles of the American Founders and the principles of early twentieth-century progressives, it's not because they're history buffs. Rather, they have a stake in believing both sets of principles, which coexist in our politics. So they can be jarred by the possibility that belief in both isn't possible.

For another thing, the American Founders were "thoughtful partisans of modernity" who understood themselves to be engaged in an experiment and who advanced their principles in the face of still living premodern alternatives. For that reason, an education that affords a central place to the respectful study of the principles of American politics makes the student aware in a way she couldn't have been before that those principles are a conscious choice.[89] Where such an education succeeds, most students, whether because even a determined attempt to educate them to respect reason's authority leaves some prejudices intact, or because the case for American political principles is good, will become more thoughtful, but not less attached, citizens. If a handful of eccentric students comes to question the goodness of the polity, we can live with, and may even benefit from, the challenge.

This confidence that the polity can survive rational scrutiny is founded on what one might call the Enlightenment gamble. We gamble on the proposition that, contrary to the experience of Socrates, who was killed by his fellow Athenians, or of Galileo, who was compelled to recant by the Church, pursuers of reason need not be simply or primarily at odds with the polity. The eighteenth-century Enlightenment took inspiration from Locke who, without making the adoption of liberal democratic premises the explicit purpose of his education, expected that an education directed toward shaping reasonable people would lead students to accept the "natural rights of men" and their natural equality.[90]

It's still appropriate to describe this confidence in reason as a bet, and a conservative might today give fewer than three cheers for the Enlightenment. But much has been built on this bet over the past few centuries, including today's colleges and universities. For this reason, conservatives who reject it are hard to distinguish from radicals.

A Conservative Challenge

I've refrained to this point from treating what I'll call anti-liberal conservatism, which does reject the Enlightenment gamble and makes a frontal assault on liberal education as I understand it. But this species of conservatism is getting a hearing today. Not only conservatives but also President Obama found much to recommend in Patrick Deneen's *Why Liberalism Failed*, a 2018 work, indeed worth reading, that sets our economic and cultural ills at the feet of Lockean liberalism.[91] To conserve liberalism is to conserve the ultimate cause of our discontents. We must "reject the belief that the ailments of liberal society can be fixed by realizing liberalism." Instead, for Deneen and conservatives of his type, "the only path to liberation from the inevitabilities and ungovernable forces that liberalism imposes is liberation from liberalism itself."[92]

On the educational scene, as we'll see in a moment, Deneen has provocatively recognized his kinship with at least one radical, a left-wing student radical, no less, and has disowned the conservatism that animates this book. Indeed, he thinks that defenders of the kind of liberal education I defend aren't conservatives at all. There's a bomb hidden in this otherwise pleasant-sounding idea of becoming a reasonable person. To tie these two thoughts together, Deneen thinks that true conservatives should agree with left-wing radicals that the liberal democratic enlightenment is poison. Any view of education that takes Locke as a starting point has started all wrong. I'll take up this challenge now.

In February 2014, a Harvard undergraduate, Sandra Korn, writing for Harvard's daily paper, the *Crimson*, decried the "liberal obsession with 'academic freedom.'"[93] The idea of academic freedom, according to Korn's argument, unrealistically suggests that campuses should distance themselves from politics in favor of the politically neutral pursuit of the truth. In attacking the idea of academic freedom, Korn is also attacking the idea I've defended in this chapter. Academic freedom, as it's understood today, means precisely that colleges and universities are devoted to following arguments wherever they lead, answering only to the dictates of "scientific conscience," or reason.[94] Academic freedom, then, is closely tied to the idea that universities are communities of reasonable people. Because such communities are worthy of protection and earn dividends, in scientific progress among other things, for polities that protect them, trustees and legislators are expected to give professors even more leeway than the First Amendment affords to other citizens.

But universities, Korn claims, can't be devoted to following arguments wherever they lead because politics are inescapable. What research gets funded and published, what topics are deemed worthy of consideration, is "always contingent on political priorities." When administrators tell protesters, "Respect that speaker's academic freedom, even though her argument gives aid and comfort to bad actors," they're really saying, "Don't challenge the status quo–hugging politics of the university." In light of the pervasiveness of politics and the phony neutrality of academic freedom, students and faculty on the left, Korn argues, should embrace a political standard, which she calls "academic justice." If, she asks, "our university community opposes racism, sexism, and heterosexism, why should we put up with research that counters our goals simply in the name of 'academic freedom'?" We shouldn't, she concludes. She's up for organizing to prevent one of Harvard's few conservative professors, Harvey Mansfield, from publishing "sexist commentary," under the "authority of a Harvard faculty position."[95] Because we conservative higher-ed writers are not above searching the pages of student newspapers for material, Korn's opinion piece drew plenty of harsh responses.

Deneen's was unusual among them in containing the sentence, "I agree with Ms. Korn."[96]

About what? First, he agrees with Korn that "academic institutions inevitably are dedicated to some substantial commitments," apart from a commitment to rational inquiry. He agrees that academic freedom masquerades as neutral, although it's a weapon. Academic freedom was the "means by which the substantial commitments once held mainly by religious institutions were initially destabilized and eventually rejected" in favor of "a new set of commitments," liberal ones. As Korn thinks that the appeal to academic freedom conceals and protects the university's conservatism, its ties to capitalism, Zionism, heterosexism, and so on, Deneen thinks that the appeal to academic freedom, or the appeal to reason, protects and masks the university's institutionalized radicalism, its disdain for religion, tradition, family, and so on.

Second, and perhaps more important, Deneen agrees with Korn that attachment to academic freedom, as it's usually understood, does nothing to improve universities. Whatever freedom an academic may enjoy must be understood in terms of and limited by a particular vision of the truth. Pope John Paul II and Benedict XVI have defended academic freedom understood in this way as "necessarily limited to efforts to better understand and articulate the truth of the Faith." But Deneen concedes that the consensus understanding of academic freedom is so far from this idea that Korn's term, "academic justice," is clearer. "I agree," Deneen says, "that we should be committed to academic justice; I disagree that today's academy has defined justice correctly." Academic justice, not the pursuit of reason untethered from specific conceptions of justice, can save us.

Let me begin by quarreling with Deneen about what academic freedom means. Deneen's problem with academic freedom is that it's connected to a broader Enlightenment effort to "liberate humans from the dead hand of the past" and ultimately from all restraint. It's a freedom that demands the dismantling of traditions on which human beings have relied for much of their history, in favor of a freedom that leads nowhere.

More broadly, Deneen thinks that Allan Bloom's understanding of liberal education, foolishly embraced by conservatives like me, is part of the problem. It "reflects a commitment to" liberty understood in a negative and therefore empty manner as "the liberation of the individual from the past and limits and place."[97] And Deneen's problem with liberal education follows from his problem with liberalism itself, which, as far back as Locke, seeks "the active liberation of the individual from any limiting conditions."[98] What could be less conservative than unmooring individuals from culture and tradition?

Deneen is right that academic freedom is not conservative in the sense of preferring tradition for tradition's sake. But it does preserve the past. As the 1915 Declaration of Principles on Academic Freedom and Academic Tenure, adopted by the American Association of University Professors, puts it, the university must be "the conservator of all genuine elements of value in the past thought and life of mankind which are not in the fashion of the moment." The university is "likely always to exercise a certain form of conservative influence" because inquirers into the truth won't worship the present, and will have a "reasonable regard for the teachings of experience."[99] This follows from the enterprise that academic freedom serves, of testing our opinions against the evidence and the best available arguments, which entails, to put it in Locke's terms, "comprehensive enlargement of mind . . . assisted with letters, and a free consideration of the several views and sentiments of thinking men of all sides."[100]

As Ruth Grant says, at least part of that enlargement of mind involves research in the humanities, returning to "old material in response to new circumstances when those circumstances cannot be adequately understood within the dominant conceptual regime." Grant calls this return "conservative" in the "rather literal sense that it depends on the conservation of the past, of the records of human action, thought, and imagination." She also calls it conservative in another sense. Studying the works of the past "produces an appreciation of the immensity of human achievement but also a recognition of the limits of human understanding and human capabilities." The study of the wisest human beings and the most advanced civilizations brings the deficiencies of all human beings and civilizations to our attention.[101] Liberal education as I've described it in this chapter is just not in league with "the active liberation of the individual from any limiting conditions."

It isn't easy to meet Deneen's exacting standard for being a conservative. In a striking column, he adopts the political theorist Herbert Storing's view that the Antifederalists, who fought the ratification of the 1787 Constitution, were "the original American conservatives." Because they've made peace with commercialism, which the Antifederalists disdained, and have become "vociferous nationalists," whereas the Antifederalists doubted the possibility of democracy on the scale of the nation, "today's conservatives are liberals."[102]

As I indicated in the preface, I join many, perhaps most, American conservatives in agreeing that I am a liberal if by liberalism one means, as Deneen does, the political philosophy, "conceived some 500 years ago," that sees "humans as rights bearing individuals" and holds that governments are instituted to "secure rights."[103] To be conservative, for Deneen, is to oppose liberalism in this sense. In truth, even the Antifederalists wouldn't count as conservatives by this standard, since, as Storing shows, the principles of the American Revolution embodied by the Declaration of Independence were among the things they wished to conserve. If they favored keeping more power at the state level than the Federalists did, it was because they saw an "inherent connection between the states and the preservation of individual liberty, which is the end of any legitimate government."[104]

This is not the time to have it out between conservatives who wish to conserve liberalism and those, like Deneen, who have been waiting five hundred years to say, "I told you so!" But we don't need to have that fight to see that Deneen's fundamental reason for separating conservatives from the idea of liberal education, that liberal education makes too many concessions to the wrong turn Europe took in the seventeenth century, relies on a rather narrow understanding of conservatism.

Even if we were to adopt Deneen's understanding of conservatism, there would be much to like in universities that seek to shape reasonable people. Universities, whatever their many defects, even today remain places in which alternatives to the prevailing views can be encountered. The Open Syllabus Project, which has collected syllabuses from more than a million courses and ranks nearly a million texts, finds Plato's *Republic* and Aristotle's *Ethics* in the top ten of assigned texts.[105] It's not true, as Deneen proposes, that the commitment to open inquiry is a mere mask for cramming the reigning opinions into unsuspecting minds. In fact, the university is one of the only places one might happen upon a serious and sustained critique of a set of political ideas that, just as Deneen says, has had hundreds of years to rout the opposition. Even my Catholic students, attached at least loosely to another ancient and troubled institution, nearly always learn for the first time when they take my course that the Church puts forward arguments, grounded not only in revelation but also in reason, for the positions it takes.

Deneen's own critique of liberalism, that it pulls us toward an impotent and shallow individualism on the one hand, and a vast administrative state on the other, is largely derived from Tocqueville. One is most likely to encounter Tocqueville as I did, in college, where, according to the Open Syllabus Project, *Democracy in America* ranks a healthy thirty-second among assigned texts. Imagine if Deneen's wish were granted and our overwhelmingly left-liberal faculties were to agree with him that they should settle on a view of "academic justice" and hire teachers and craft syllabuses accordingly. Suppose they were to cast caution aside, recognizing that professionalism is no more neutral than academic freedom itself, and fully devote themselves to advancing social justice through their teaching and research. Presumably, the stranglehold of liberalism, and the left-wing views that Deneen considers predictable outcomes of liberalism, would only tighten.

In any case, the success of the Enlightenment gamble, which is also Locke's gamble, doesn't culminate in a human being or citizen who knows no limits. To subject oneself to the authority of reason, to feel pride in obeying it and shame in abandoning it, is to accept a limit. That is one reason why, in Plato's *Republic*, engaging in dialogue is at times presented as an obligation, "for the argument is not just any question but about the way one should live."[106] Even the man Socrates is talking to here, Thrasymachus, who acts as if he considers reason simply a means of getting the better of others, isn't deaf to the plea that a human being should try to live within the limits of reason, rather than willfully refuse all limits. When Locke sternly says that there's no worse failing for anyone who claims to be rational than not to yield to reason, he works within the Socratic tradition, one that subjects human beings to limits.

This tradition isn't wholly conservative in any sense of the term. Once we're brought to examine and test our own principles, however much we might imagine that reality has a conservative bias, we may discover that those principles are unsound. But as Buckley saw in considering Allan Bloom's work, the mere determination to take arguments seriously, in an atmosphere otherwise hostile to conservative principles, is of great value.

And at a deeper level, shouldn't a conservative be at least as satisfied as a liberal when a student feels the sting of the injunction to keep pursuing the argument, "for the argument is not just any question but about the way one should live"? That's the quotation that I—and I'm hardly original in this—put at the head of my syllabus for the Common Intellectual Experience, among the first courses students take at Ursinus, which focuses on fundamental, enduring questions that human beings can encounter in nearly all times and places. Yes, I'm a conservative, but I can't think of any strain of conservatism that wants young people to be frivolous about serious matters.

CHAPTER FOUR

Shaping Reasonable Students

Spend enough time on campus and some cynic will tell you that college is terrific, except for all the students. Nonetheless, especially as we're fed a diet of stories about today's students— some find them heroic, others irredeemable—those of us who propose aims for higher education have to reckon with the students whom we aim to highly educate. My reckoning may be less satisfying than some others in that my conclusion is mainly negative: we professors know less than we think we know about our students. If we hope to have reasonable students, we need to be more reasonable about them. So I'll make a case for hope but will also try to remain mindful that a man of fifty-one is in danger of making a fool of himself when he claims to speak knowledgeably about the young.

The Unbearable Opacity of Students

Last chapter, we heard from Ruth Grant that judgment is needed because "the world always remains opaque to us in important respects." Some things that matter to us are also stubbornly complex and ambiguous, even after all the arguments have been weighed. This is also an insight of conservatism as I understand it.

But when Grant says the world remains opaque to "us" in important respects, that "us" includes teachers and that world includes students. What can we know about the stubbornly complex and ambiguous human beings whom we teach?

We'd like to know much. We assume that our students' judgment is in some ways enhanced and in other ways spoiled by presuppositions, penchants, and passions of which they're not fully aware. This is, to use Plato's simile, their cave. We suspect that life in this cave, though healthy in some ways, is unhealthy in others, and that being cut off from reflection on one's presuppositions, penchants, and passions stunts one's growth. So already, teachers should know a lot about what their students believe and care about—what kind of cave they're in. And we should know something about what non-stunted growth—or human flourishing—is, and how our students can be helped to have a share in it.

But teachers can't take it for granted that they know these things about their students. Parents rarely know their own children as well as that, even though they observe them from birth and typically have a small number to monitor. Even so, how often does a well-intentioned intervention, not because of some prejudice the parent has but because of incomplete knowledge, go wrong? That's never happened to me, but I've read about it in the parenting literature.

Further, teachers, like everyone else, are prejudiced, subject to, among other stupidities, confirmation bias—the tendency to look for and interpret evidence to back up our preconceived notions. We are also prone, more than most, I'd guess, to overconfidence. We frequently appeal, in disputes with our colleagues, to what "the students" say or think, without considering that the students we know may be unrepresentative, or that our students may be telling us what we want to hear, or that we may be hard of hearing. A colleague of mine once claimed, sincerely I think, that her students had, unprompted, voiced their approval of a change in the way we were handling a course. The change had taken place a decade earlier, long before any of those students had enrolled. They could not, unprompted, have been aware of it, much less have had an informed opinion. A defective but common feedback loop was likely at work: we directly or indirectly let students in on what we think; they later repeat it back to us; we run to our colleagues armed with this evidence of what "the students" believe.

In *Why Higher Education Should Have a Leftist Bias*, Donald Lazere performs this move on a grand scale. With five decades of teaching experience to lend his words weight, he says that students refuse "to see beyond their personal experience." Their families didn't own slaves, they reason. They aren't prejudiced, they suppose. Therefore, the problem of race prejudice in America must be grossly exaggerated.[1] No doubt, Lazere has heard a non-trivial number of students voice some version of the view that racial discrimination is no longer a major problem in America. So have I. But the Higher Education Research Institute (HERI) asks large numbers of entering freshmen most years whether they agree or disagree that "racial discrimination is no longer a major problem in America." Year after year, few— just 17.1% in the 2017 survey—agree even somewhat.[2]

Lazere might counter that things are different for the "Middle American whites" he has dealt with at the non-elite universities he has known.[3] These places, he'd have us believe, are packed with Dittoheads and aspiring Ann Coulters. But that's unlikely. The HERI Freshman Survey slices the higher education pie into

numerous pieces—public, private, religious, non-sectarian, and
more. In 2017, no subgroup broke 18% on the racial discrimination question. Either Lazere is hyper-attuned to a minority
view, or his students are atypical, in which case his work should
have been entitled, *Why Higher Education in Unusual Classrooms Like Mine Should Have a Leftist Bias.*

Making false assumptions about students can cause otherwise conscientious teachers to take wrong turns. Lazere's teaching strategy proceeds from his narrow understanding of what
his students' prejudices are. Like me, he wants to practice "liberal education," which entails "broadening students' perspectives beyond those of their upbringing." But he also thinks that
many students are "limited in their political views to the conservative commonplaces" they've "heard from their parents
and peers."[4]

Getting down to the genesis of these commonplaces, Lazere
argues that America has suffered and still suffers from "a con-
tinuous series of political and cultural offensives, engineered by
the Republican Party and its allies since the 1970s."[5] Compliant
media figures corrupted by wealth, and left-liberal leaders, "in-
toxicated by the sweet smell of success," reinforce the "deliber-
ate social control, propaganda, polemics, and semantic agenda-
setting" that hold up the "conservative status quo."[6]

Consequently, to broaden student minds, Lazere proposes
that classes in argumentative rhetoric should give "a full accounting of [the sins] of the right," while considering the "best
conservative rebuttals" available.[7] If the remainder of Lazere's
book is any indication, rhetoric courses will henceforth consist
in reading and exposing the hypocrisy of Irving Kristol, Nor-
man Podhoretz, and other neoconservative figures with whom
Lazere has long-standing beefs.

If you see a virtually all-powerful corporate conservative cabal hiding behind the Democratic Party, the news media, and other seemingly left-leaning American institutions, then you might think that liberal education requires a frontal assault on the cabal's best hypnotists. You won't be fooled, as Lazere evidently isn't, by the fact that—to return to HERI's Freshman Survey—students have complicated political views. In 2015, more than 70% of incoming freshmen agreed that "colleges should prohibit racist/sexist speech on campus." Eighty-one percent agreed that "same-sex couples should have the right to legal marital status." On the other hand, only a bare majority agreed that "students from disadvantaged social backgrounds should be given preferential treatment in college admissions."[8] In 2017, when, as we've seen, only a small minority denied the salience of racial discrimination, a comfortable majority, nearly 70%, agreed that "through hard work, everybody can succeed in American society."[9] Jean Twenge, the psychologist and expert on generational differences, reviewing a range of evidence, finds both libertarian and socialist streaks in the new generation that she has dubbed iGen (others call it Generation Z), about which we're about to hear more.[10] Students tilt left-liberal but don't fit snugly into any political box.

Never mind, though; Lazere has met and taught a lot of rubes.

Generation ZZZZZ

Survey data of the sort HERI gathers can check some of our biases. But in thinking about my classroom, I don't put much stock in surveys, especially when they're used to divide students into generations.

Early in my career, a *Chronicle of Higher Education* writer advised us, in the manner of a square delivering a lecture on hipness, that most American college students were raised on, sniff, "the institution known as 'MTV.'" When they gazed up from "quick edits, contemporary music, and dazzling dance routines," they demanded "warp-speed answers to their life issues." Who were we, then, not to rejigger our syllabuses to clarify what our courses had to do with their careers? They were used to innovative camera, lighting, and set design work, blended to create a visual and auditory story of teen angst or joy. No problem. We had electronic whiteboards and PowerPoint. If we used tech tools judiciously, we could "remain both the intellectual and the technological leaders of our classrooms," the masters of our pedagogical domains. Above all, we mustn't cross the kids, whom we were to picture, with remote in hand, poised to change the channel. We were advised to gauge their present mood via "opinion pulses."[11]

The terms that describe the generations change. The advice mostly doesn't. In 2016, *InsideHigherEd* published an advice column that informed readers that members of a heretofore undiscovered species, millennials "have a shorter attention span" than the average Labrador retriever, and "are driven by instant gratification." But, straighten your pith helmet and dive in because they can be lured into your pedagogical trap with "video clips [a link directs us to TED talks], podcasts" and other baits. Just be sure to "deliver knowledge in small doses: Ten minutes is as long as you'll be able to hold a Millennial's interest. So keep switching every ten minutes." One might try a "ten-minute anecdote, followed by a short video." Try exploring "microlearning."[12]

Reader, I didn't try to explore it.

And now we have Generation Z, or iGen. Its members need "e-textbooks with videos, interactive figures, and built-in quizzes." The videos that they "watch online are rarely more than three minutes long," so who do we think we're kidding when we ask them to concentrate on books?[13]

This is where the pedagogical wisdom of the past two decades, otherwise divergent, converges. More videos. Shorter, please.

Let's be fair to Jean Twenge, who makes that e-textbook recommendation. She's right that sensible teachers "meet [students] where they are."[14] Twenge doesn't recommend that we stop asking our students to read challenging books. Rather, we may have to build up to *War and Peace*, or even to long magazine articles. Fair enough. As Twenge documents, what students say about their reading habits supports professors, who might otherwise be dismissed as nostalgics, when they gripe that students are less interested in and practiced at reading than they were two decades ago. Students weren't great readers then, either, but one can't help but be deflated by this finding of HERI's 2015 Freshman Survey: 58.2% of incoming freshmen reported spending one hour or less per week reading for pleasure during the previous year. In 1995, the high but marginally less soul-crushing figure was 48.7%.[15]

Even if we take the data at face value, however, they don't tell us how to reach our students. Recall Mark Edmundson. His students find him "enjoyable." He's down with "current culture" and, consequently, students find even Sigmund Freud "interesting" when Edmundson delivers Freud's heavy ideas in the manner, as Edmundson's title puts it, of "lite entertainment." But Edmundson thinks his students can do more than enjoy the works he teaches much the way they might enjoy a middling

TV series. They can be challenged, inspired—perhaps changed—by the works he teaches, even if they haven't been challenged, inspired, or changed by books before. Edmundson vows that "when the kids' TV-based tastes come to the fore, [he'll] aim and shoot." And "when it comes time to praise genius . . . [he'll] try to do it in the right style, full-out, with faith that finer artistic spirits (maybe not Homer and Isaiah quite, but close, close), still alive somewhere in the ether will help [him] out."[16]

So the cultural odds are loaded, as one suspects they've always been, against the best kind of teaching. Nonetheless, I doubt Edmundson's buying it when he's told, as a recent *Chronicle of Higher Education* advice column told all of us old-timers, that one had best assign "a maximum of two five-page articles for any one class." That's not because he's crotchety, or hasn't noticed that some students fake their way through class discussions, but rather because he thinks that genius can swim upstream. Contrary to the column's author, assigning more than ten minutes of reading is not mere "virtue-signaling to other professors," even though, yeah, yeah, yeah, it's a "digital age."[17]

Some Almost Permanent Things

Again, Edmundson doesn't deny that things change; his article is largely about students brought up in a consumer culture that hasn't always existed. However, he banks on the likelihood—never denied by generational storm spotters—that many things don't change. Perhaps Edmundson's confidence is increased, as mine is, by the way in which ancient philosophy and literature resonate with some of our students, even though they aren't members of—what?—Generation Beta?

Although I admire the innovative and informative work of Jean Twenge, an old University of Chicago acquaintance (Burton Judson represent!), I'm suspicious of it, too. I don't believe her interview subject, "Melissa," when she says, "I couldn't care less how I am viewed by society. I live my life according to the morals, views, and standards that I create." She is, I think, putting herself and us on. I doubt that her comment represents a "revolution," in which Melissa's "Generation Me," "those born 1970 to 1999," are swept up, that is greatly diminishing the otherwise reliable human tendency to care about what other people think. Fine, the young people Twenge profiled are more inclined to dress down at work than their predecessors were. But it hardly seems likely that they're beyond making "a good impression on others" and trying to "elicit their approval." Maybe Melissa wears custom distressed jeans when she utters the sort of statement Twenge reports and maybe she doesn't. But the Gap wouldn't offer an array of ripped and distressed jeans if the young were now dressing just to be "relaxed, natural, and happy."[18]

Rousseau noticed that his sophisticated French fellow intellectuals had "natural" and "easy" manners and that they affected to despise "public opinion." But he also noticed that, if anything, they cared more about what other people thought of them than less sophisticated people did.[19] They exemplified, for Rousseau, a general characteristic of civilized people. Civilized man, partly because of his economic dependence on others and partly because he can't escape their gaze, "knows how to live only in the opinion of others," drawing even "the sentiment of his own existence" from "their judgment alone."[20] Perhaps this portrait is hyperbolic. But it's going to take a lot more evidence than we've got now to persuade me that a new generation has overcome shame. And when someone protests that he doesn't care what other people think of him, I suspect he cares a lot.

Indeed, although the first edition of Twenge's *Generation Me*, which appeared in 2006, didn't deal with social media, the revised edition introduces us to "Chloe," an eighteen-year-old who says, "I have almost 10,000 followers and many of my friends are not even at 1,000. . . . I guess I enjoy portraying my life as fabulous."[21] Few will dispute Twenge's judgment that this statement is narcissistic. But Twenge doesn't dwell on one conclusion we can draw from it. As much as young people might bravely say, along with Melissa, that they don't care what others think, they probably, like Chloe, care desperately about what others think.[22] Anyone who has taken a horrified glance at Facebook knows that for adults and young people alike, living in and through the opinion of others didn't go out with bell-bottoms. Getting this right is no small thing. As I hope I indicated in chapter 3, we misunderstand our students, and throw away one of our best tools, if we imagine they have overcome shame.

On the other hand, I'm with Twenge when she says that Generation Me and iGen, those "born in 1995 and later," are deeply individualistic.[23] The sociologist Robert Bellah and his co-authors worried about this trend more than thirty years ago.[24] The political scientist Robert Putnam had us all talking, twenty years ago, about how we now bowl alone.[25] And in observing that modern currents pull us apart, Putnam and Bellah followed Tocqueville, who was on to us in this respect almost two hundred years ago. Tocqueville saw, as he looked at nineteenth-century Europe and America, that democracy was undoing an aristocratic order, in which one's way of life and ties to others were dictated by one's place in a natural or divine hierarchy. As that order receded, the individual increasingly tended to "withdraw to one side with his family and his friends" and to "seek the reason for things by [himself] and in [himself] alone."[26] We conservatives aren't ones to jump on a trend, but we'll concede, now that it has been around for centuries, that individualism is probably not a fad.

From a Toquevillian perspective, it's not surprising that individualism is on the rise today, as the resources Tocqueville found pushing against it, in religion, civic associations, and local government, all seem diminished. None of this is a knock on Twenge, who agrees that individualism has been increasing for "perhaps even several centuries."[27] I mean only to say that, like our anxiety about what others—from our friends to Twitter randos—think of us, democratic individualism and its implications aren't going away soon. We can count on them.

These implications are—I know I've used these words before but it wouldn't be bad to tattoo them to our fists—complex and ambiguous. Twenge's data suggest that Generation Me undergraduates, despite their individualism, believed more than their predecessors "that their lives were controlled by outside forces." This finding at first seems at odds with their individualism. "If GenMe'ers see themselves as independent individuals, why are they increasingly blaming others when things go wrong?" Twenge speculates that for GenMe students, whose self-esteem was off the charts, one way to make sense of failure, which couldn't possibly be their fault, was to curse fate.[28]

Tocqueville suggests, on the other hand, that a low estimate of one's ability to control things is an old democratic illness that doesn't contradict but rather follows from individualism. When fixed hierarchies dissolve, and the democratic individual compares himself to others, he "feels with pride that he is the equal of each of them." Who are they to tell him what to think or do? But his isolation also has the effect of making him feel anxious and weak. When he compares himself to the majority, he "is immediately overwhelmed by his own insignificance." To that majority, he promptly cedes his mind and will. Similarly, democratic historians "attribute almost no influence to the individual over the destiny of the species" because when "all citizens are independent of one another, and each of them is weak," "individuals seem absolutely powerless" to make history.[29] When the shackles of the old order are removed, one feels free, but when one's bonds to others are broken, one feels small. No wonder that, late in the democratic day, we find people flexing in one snapshot and freaking out in another.

Tocqueville's explanation doesn't exclude Twenge's, and I doubt one could prove either by poring over survey data. Such data, though they may lead us to question our assumptions about students, don't tell us what students think. It doesn't take a psychoanalyst to imagine that a person's deepest concerns may be hidden from view. And if a survey happens to reveal what students think, it may not tell us to what extent they care, why they think what they do, or how one thought might be qualified or contradicted by other thoughts. Even asking directly, whether in a classroom or non-classroom setting, only helps so much because it's hard to be confident that you're hearing a student's actual views. Perhaps what's needed, at our colleges and universities, is not another workshop on Generation Z, conducted by generously compensated gurus, but rather alertness to our tendency to think we know our students when we don't.

That's not to say that we lack resources in this matter any more than a parent is completely at sea in knowing a child, or a friend is completely at sea in knowing a friend. In more than twenty years of teaching, for example, I've never felt misled by Allan Bloom's observation that "almost every student entering the university believes, or says he believes, that truth is relative." And I've never felt misled by his less noticed observation that almost every student also has a non-relativistic "allegiance to equality" that runs deeper than that student's relativism.[30] Relativism, the view that there is no truth but only multiple subjective opinions, is "not a theoretical insight but a moral postulate" that supports equality. As long as no way of life or opinion is superior to any other, no person can be superior to any other. That is why even students otherwise shy about the idea of evil will react to racism, sexism, and other inegalitarian -isms with anger, as evils, rather than as subjective opinions among other equally valid subjective opinions. One finds the force of this egalitarian relativism in strange places. A student of mine, during a discussion of Genesis, proclaimed that the Bible should be read as the literal word of God. She quickly added that this was merely her personal opinion.

I don't doubt that students today are different in some respects from the students I taught at the beginning of my career in the late 1990s. On average, for example, students now seem to be less religious and more beset by mental health issues than they were.[31] But, for whatever my testimony is worth, students, in their propensity to worry about what others think of them, or their individualism, or their love of equality, or their relativism, seem now about as they seemed way back then.

At least as important, I don't think they're worse or better, from the standpoint of their capacity to become reasonable, than the human beings Locke had in front of him in the seventeenth century. The very "inclinations of our nature," Locke asserts, "dispose us to a right use of our understandings." The mind "no sooner entertains any proposition, but it presently hastens to some hypothesis to bottom it on." What's more, Locke thinks that we care whether that hypothesis is true or not. So that when our "false maxims are brought to the test" and fail, we will "acknowledge them to be fallible," if only temporarily.[32] Students still find it unsettling when they're caught in a contradiction, or when two things they want to believe in and act on—say the lessons of Machiavelli and the lessons of Christ—appear to contradict each other.

But hastening to anchor our ideas on solid ground can work against us. As Locke goes on to explain, our haste causes us to rely "upon testimony" when it shouldn't be relied on, "because it is easier to believe than to be scientifically instructed."[33] The ground we find may be "true or false, solid or sandy." That we are "unquiet or unsettled" before we cast anchor suggests that we may not be in a frame of mind to make sure we're anchoring someplace secure. To the unquiet and unsettled person, a conspiracy theory, or any wrongheaded theory that lets him imagine he has a handle on things, may look solid. Even if you convince him of his error, by showing him evidence against his theory, you may find him, "the very next occasion that offers, argu[ing] again on the same grounds."

I'd be surprised if anyone reading this book hasn't been puzzled or annoyed by the way in which refutations, accepted in the moment, somehow don't stick. Locke says that's the way it is with us when we aren't in the habit of examining our premises. Although people "would be intolerable to themselves ... if they [were to] embrace opinions without any ground, and hold what they could give no manner of reason for," and are consequently open to reason, they also readily abandon or turn against it. The inclinations of our nature, now as back then, put us in a position to become reasonable people, but they don't make it easy.[34]

Are Our Students Safetyists?

Yet, to return to Generation Z, despite these permanent or nearly permanent attributes of students, which give us much to work with, people both inside and outside of colleges love to play "Guess what's new about students today." We'll probably guess wrong. As with our attempts to speak the language of the

young, or to keep up with social media technology, we're usually two steps behind when we try to describe our students.
Apparently, they're no longer on MySpace.

If you were thinking about students in 2014, you probably
thought that students weren't interested enough in politics. You
may have noticed them perk up in advance of and in the immediate aftermath of President Obama's election, but that
bump didn't last far into his first term, as "We are the ones we've
been waiting for" gave way to the dull business of governing.
You may also have agreed with Arthur Levine and Diane R.
Dean, the authors of *Generation on a Tightrope*, that students
then had "less interest in . . . campus activism than their predecessors," that race was no more central an issue than parking in
what protests there were, and that building takeovers were
largely a thing of the past. Students then, unlike students before,
were too apathetic to fight the powers that be.[35] That's the impression one might have gotten from a "snapshot of US undergraduates enrolled between 2005 and 2014."[36]

The snapshot may well have been good, but in the 2015–16
school year, you'd have consigned it to the flames, as, starting at
the University of Missouri, protests, largely focused on issues
of race and surprisingly indifferent to parking, spread across the
country. By December 2015, activists had hammered out demands at more than fifty schools.[37] Politics on campus were
suddenly supercharged.

Jonathan Haidt and Greg Lukianoff, in their influential book,
The Coddling of the American Mind, have tried to make sense of
these developments—particularly the attitude of student activists toward speech—in terms of generational change. Lukianoff
noticed, around 2013, that moves to censor speech, which had
typically come from college administrators, were now coming
from students. Demands to censor speech also came with a new

justification, that speech jeopardized students' mental health by making them feel unsafe. Safety, "gradually, in the twenty-first century, on some college campuses . . . underwent a process of 'concept creep' and expanded to include emotional safety." By a similar process, words, not only epithets hurled by malicious people who might follow up with physical violence, but also academic journal articles written by mild-mannered, well-meaning philosophers, came to be seen as violent.[38] No wonder, Lukianoff and Haidt suggest, students resorted to physical violence to shut down speech at Middlebury College and University of California, Berkeley in 2017. Why shouldn't violence beget violence?[39]

Conveniently, iGen entered college right around 2013, when Lukianoff noticed things changing, and Jean Twenge says that its members are "obsessed with safety." She confirms, too, that iGen-ers believe that "one should be safe not just from car accidents and sexual assault but from people who disagree with you."[40] Lukianoff, Haidt, and Twenge agree that iGen's obsession with safety has to do with a wider cultural emphasis on safety: "iGen's was the childhood . . . of being picked up at school instead of walking home by yourself, of sanitized plastic playgrounds."[41] Too "much close supervision and protection can morph into safetyism," the view that safety trumps all other considerations.[42] When overprotected children leave home for college, they "feel unprotected and vulnerable" and try "to re-create that feeling of home and safety that they [had] just a few months before."[43] Because young people have learned that the world is a dangerous place, full of menacing strangers and defective playground equipment, they consider themselves, and in some ways really are, fragile.

I'm a fan of *The Coddling of the American Mind*, which proposes that we help young people shed the cognitive distortions endemic to safetyism and, yes, to become reasonable people.[44] Higher education leaders should heed Lukianoff and Haidt, who urge universities to tie their identities, deliberately and publicly, to rational inquiry. However, I find Lukianoff and Haidt's explanation of how we got here unconvincing.

Don't get me wrong. There's evidence for their thesis that students, and not administrators, are driving demands for censorship. For example, it wasn't administrators, but seventy-five students, who marched into a University of California, Berkeley class and shouted "Bullshit!" at a professor who had criticized the university's affirmative action program. When a professor of French produced a "kind of French language TV soap opera" as a teaching aid, it wasn't Yale University's administrators who complained that the "sexist heterosexual romance" was "very offensive," or that bald people might be hurt by the discussion of "hair vocabulary," or that the video as a whole constituted sexual harassment. Those were Yale students, seemingly driven by the humanitarian but speech-unfriendly conviction that "wrongheaded opinions are harsh and harsh words are hurtful." And there is, it's true, a worrying trend toward seeing "hurtful words [as] a form of violence," and claiming that "painful criticism is violence." All this can end with an "erasure of the distinction . . . between discussion and bloodshed," with the corollary that violent speech can be met with physical violence.

That's exactly what Lukianoff and Haidt are talking about. But it's also all out of Jonathan Rauch's 1993 book, *Kindly Inquisitors*, which was itself describing the atmosphere on campus when I, a card-carrying member of Generation X, was finishing college.[45] Even if Haidt and Lukianoff and Twenge are right that iGen differs dramatically from previous generations, the campus politics they're describing resemble the campus politics of my late lamented youth. There is little new here, which is why we shouldn't dissect the new generation in search of causes.

If we decide to focus on iGen anyway, we don't find much support for the Lukianoff-Haidt-Twenge thesis. Are we dealing with a generation obsessed with safety? Twenge gives us a striking chart, drawing on data from the University of Michigan's Monitoring the Future Survey. Eighth and tenth graders agree nowadays, markedly less than they did from 1991 to 2009, that they "like to take risks sometimes" and "get a kick out of doing dangerous things." The chart is striking because the numbers seem to fall off a cliff around 2009. Recall that iGen starts around 1995, so the timing is right.[46]

However, Twenge's chart begins in 1991. In 2015, Katherine Keyes, a professor of epidemiology at Columbia University's Mailman School of Public Health, and her co-authors noted, also based on Monitoring the Future data, that "preference for risky activities has increased among adolescents in the US, especially among young women."[47] It took a leap during the 1980s, and by 1991, when Twenge's chart begins, it was sharply up from where it had been in the early 1980s, when my Gen-X cohort was moving through middle school and high school. We were known, by the way, not only for our collective crush on Molly Ringwald but also for our desire "to avoid risk, pain and rapid change."[48]

So yes, the percentage of eighth and tenth graders who gave risk-loving answers to certain survey questions took a plunge around 2009. But that plunge was from a height. We have a way to go yet before we get to the risk aversion of the early 1980s. In 1982, twelfth graders[49] were as likely to disagree as to agree with the statement, "I like to test myself every now and then by doing something a little risky." They were considerably more likely to disagree than to agree with the statement, "I get a kick out of doing things that are a little dangerous." They were, then, considerably more risk-averse by this measure than twelfth graders in 2017 who were, by a good margin, more likely to agree than to disagree with both statements.[50] Yet, I can attest, high schoolers in the early 1980s had been pretty much raised by wolves, permitted to ride beltless in the backs of station wagons, and to run alone to school with scissors. So the data don't fit the hypothesis that iGen's risk tolerance is uncommonly low, or that the dip after 2009 has to do with their overprotected upbringings.[51]

In fairness to Lukianoff and Haidt, their explanation of campus trends is complex and includes factors, such as political polarization, that have nothing to do with risk tolerance. But the obsession with safety they attribute to iGen in particular is, for them, arguably the most important cause of those trends, which, they say, didn't really pick up until "the last of the Millennials graduated to be replaced by iGen."[52]

In any case, the "coddling" was in place well before iGen arrived. Levine and Dean considered overprotective parenting to be a leading influence on the characters of the students, mostly millennials, whom they studied. This—here they're approvingly quoting a student affairs professional—"is a generation that was never permitted to skin their knees. They all won awards at everything they ever tried." Millennials are beneficiaries of grade inflation. They have helicopter parents, like the one who, according to a beleaguered administrator, "called a total of fifteen times one afternoon to reach me, our CFO, and the president to discuss the difficulty her son was having with his wireless Internet connection."[53] These millennials, who were risk-tolerant and whose campuses were calm, have had roughly the same "coddling" as iGen-ers, who are less risk-tolerant and whose campuses are explosive.

As for the generation or generations that didn't skin their knees, I suspect we give the attempt to shield children from harm too much credit. I'm a parent, familiar with participation trophies and not keeping score. But children aren't stupid. At every children's sporting event I've attended, however pointedly the adults pretended not to know who was winning and by how much, the kids knew exactly what the score was. If there was a single child who didn't know the difference between winning a championship and receiving a participation trophy, I never encountered him. At my children's elementary school, although students were encouraged never to refer to the gifted program as the gifted program, they called it the gifted program anyway. Perhaps more important, whatever attempt parents make to spare their children—and we certainly can be overprotective—children do skin their knees, bomb tests, get dumped, fail to make the A team, and so on. They aren't strangers to disappointment.

It would be foolish to deny that there are real generational differences between my grandparents, my parents, me, and my children. But we shouldn't be confident we have a handle on those differences, and we should try not to underestimate the intelligence of today's young people. Even Lukianoff and Haidt, who are careful not to blame college students for their faults, fall into the opposite error of treating them like hapless victims of misguided adults.

Trying to Be Reasonable About Speech

As we've already noticed, a knock against "kids today" is their disdain for free speech. But here, too, we may be underestimating them. Their views on speech, likely not as different from recent cohorts as some fear, are mixed, and where they are skeptical of untrammeled speech, they are sometimes on to something. Whatever the merit of the argument that we make progress through the free exchange of ideas, colleges can't claim to fulfill their missions merely by setting the conditions for such an exchange and leaving students to wander in the marketplace of ideas. Yet our debate concerning speech on campus focuses mainly on who has a right to say what, without due attention to what students have to gain and how they get in a position to gain by listening.

Some students live up to their billing as disdainers of free speech. There's no defending the student activists who shut down Heather Mac Donald at Claremont College in the spring of 2017. Mac Donald a mainstream, if sharp-elbowed, conservative, was scheduled to give a lecture there, drawing on her book, *The War on Cops*. Student activists, describing Mac Donald as a "notorious white supremacist fascist," organized to stop her from being heard. They blocked the entrance to the building where Mac Donald was to speak. She gave her talk, which was live-streamed, to a nearly empty hall, as protesters chanted and banged on the windows. The question and answer session was cut short, and Mac Donald was "hustled" out, like a witness against the mob, under police protection, through the building's kitchen, and into a waiting unmarked van.[54]

The Foundation for Individual Rights in Education (FIRE)—Greg Lukianoff is its president—tracks attempts to disinvite or shut down speakers. The year before the Mac Donald incident, the Disinvitation Database logged a record number of attempts. The second-highest number was recorded in 2017. The numbers, forty-three and thirty-six, weren't crisis numbers. But they suggested a trend. If you want to pin that trend on Generation Z, you're in luck. The average number of attempts from 2013 to 2017, thirty-two, was much higher than the average from 2008 to 2012, twenty-one.[55]

But in other respects, the timing is wrong. Students are more open to banning speakers they consider extreme than they were at one time, but that change was fully in evidence well before iGen hit campus. A number of surveys look at student attitudes toward speech. We don't have the luxury to examine them all. But consider the Higher Education Research Institute's Freshman Survey again, which samples far more students than the others. One question asks students to what extent they agree that colleges have a right to ban extreme speakers from campus. Starting off at a relative high of 37.2% agreement in 1967, agreement stuck between 20% and 25% from 1972 to 1986, when HERI stopped asking the question for a while. When HERI started asking again, in 2004, things had changed dramatically. Agreement was now in the low forties, where it has remained. Because of the fifteen-year gap in the data, we don't know whether the climb was gradual or sudden and can't come near pinpointing its cause. But we do have good evidence of a change in attitudes toward campus speech that was mostly accomplished by 2004.[56]

Even where surveys find worrying news for us free speech warriors, they suggest that students may be open to argument. A survey commissioned by FIRE found a majority of student respondents agreeing that "colleges and universities should be able to restrict student expression of political views that are hurtful or offensive to certain students." A majority—and this holds up for Democrats, Republicans, and Independents—also agreed that "it is important to be part of a campus community where I am not exposed to intolerant or offensive ideas." That's worrying. On the other hand, healthy majorities of all political persuasions agreed that "students should have the right to free speech on campus, even if what they are saying offends others." And when asked about Charlottesville, a majority agreed that

"white nationalists should be allowed to protest peacefully."
Students are of at least two minds about restricting campus
speech.[57]

In a 2016 Knight / Newseum survey, the vast majority of college students agreed that colleges and universities should be
able to restrict "costumes that stereotype certain racial or ethnic
groups." But an even larger majority, in contrast to FIRE's finding, disagreed that colleges and universities should be able to
restrict "expressing political views that are upsetting or offensive to certain groups." Finally, when given a choice between
having an open environment, even if that means offending certain groups of people, and having a positive environment, even
if that means restricting speech, 78% of student respondents
chose an open environment, a larger majority than Knight /
Newseum found in its adult sample.[58]

The best characterization of student opinion on free speech
is that it's conflicted. My own experience, when I co-taught a
course on free speech in 2018, was that students could shift from
a view highly favorable to free speech to a view highly unfavor-
able to it and back again in the course of a single class session.
There's reason to believe that they're open to arguments.

But how good are the arguments we make for free speech on
campus?

One argument draws on John Stuart Mill, author of the 1859
work, *On Liberty*. The usual First Amendment kinds of arguments for free speech aren't great fits for universities, which are
more concerned with the pursuit of truth and the cultivation of
judgment than they are with beating back the coercive power
of the state. Mill is a better fit. He argues that human beings are
bad judges, in large part because for us, "one-sidedness has always been the rule."[59] We're natural partisans, who grasp one
piece of the truth and mistake it for the whole truth. What saves

us from this defect is that we're capable of correcting ourselves. But our one-sidedness can be corrected only by exposure to "every variety of opinion" and way of looking at things. "No wise man," Mill says, "ever acquired his wisdom in any mode but this."[60]

That is perhaps the leading argument for free speech on campus: free speech is essential to the pursuit of the truth.

This argument suggests that truth-seeking requires "the reconciling and combining of opposites."[61] That's the sound motive for demanding "balance" in how colleges and universities treat controversial issues. If you're inviting a Republican to campus, you should also invite a Democrat. If you invite a liberal, you should invite a conservative. If we hear from an anti-Israel speaker, we should hear from a pro-Israel one. The university, on this interpretation, is akin to a public park in which you've got the Trumpists handing out leaflets in one corner, and the Resistance handing them out in another. We'll read both and figure it out.

But even Mill doesn't think that many of us will figure it out. He anticipates that when people find out what others think, most will become more rather than less one-sided. "I acknowledge," he says, "that the tendency of all opinions to become sectarian is not cured by the freest discussion but is often heightened and exacerbated thereby." When I didn't know about the other opinion, I could ignore it, but now I reject it "all the more violently" because I see it "proclaimed by persons," living, breathing people whom I can regard as hateful "opponents." Why does Mill think this outcome, which sounds terrible, is alright? He says, "It is not on the impassioned partisan" but "on the calmer and more disinterested bystander that the collision of opinions works its salutary effect."[62]

In other words, sure, if I invite a pro-Trump and an anti-Trump speaker to campus, most of us will have more foam in our mouths than we did before. But a calmer and more disinterested bystander—I'm picturing someone in tweed—can stand there with a clipboard as we yell and throw things at each other, nod his head sagely, and say to himself, "This is very interesting indeed."

How strange that students aren't bowled over by this argument.

Free Speech Is an Acquired Taste

Students who are skeptical about the value of untrammeled free speech have reasons to be skeptical.[63] The examples of speech we have in front of us are, on average, uninspiring. If you watch spin doctors work on TV, or spend an hour in the company of Twitter blowhards, you could easily get the impression that speech is mainly a way, short of force, to get what you want, or to show off. In the classroom, our students may well have observed successful, glib, students, sometimes unprepared for class, putting their teachers on to earn a good grade in participation. Our political debates, characterized by phony rage and bad faith disagreement about the facts under discussion, make it easy to understand why a sensible and well-meaning person might think, "Would it be so bad if some of these people were forced, sometimes, just a little, to shut up?"—particularly if their speech appears to be harming others.

We might be able to convince such a sensible and well-meaning person not to shut other people up by forgetting about Mill and appealing to standard and persuasive arguments for free speech. We might tell her, for example, that attempts to shut down bad speech often result in the suppression of good speech. College administrators don't have the power that states have, but one might still be leery about granting them much discretion over what can and can't be said. We might tell her that the best remedy for bad speech is counter-speech. But that point of view stays within the terms I've just described. It merely says to people who want their view to prevail that they're wrong if they imagine that suppressing speech is a well-calculated means to that end. Speech remains a mere means of advancing one's opinion or interest, to be restricted in the event my cost-benefit analysis changes.

If students, or non-students, are to learn something when they find themselves, as both Mill and Locke counsel them to, looking at a variety of opinions, they have to be convinced that there's a kind of speech other than the kind that's an instrument for overcoming others or puffing oneself up. They have to experience the kind of speech by means of which people who share an interest in the truth, and a willingness to live according to what they can see of it, test and learn from each other. If the "calmer and more disinterested bystander" is the one who can benefit from observing a clash of opposing arguments, then our students have to see some value in being, at least for a time, above that fray, and in distinguishing between sages and hucksters. In other words, we have to initiate them into the kind of community I described in chapter 3, of people who pride themselves on following the evidence and arguments where they lead, and who share at least provisional standards for evaluating evidence and arguments, even in matters that can't be definitively settled.

A member of such a community may or may not turn out to be a defender of free speech in the same way or to the same extent that the most recent decisions of the US Supreme Court suggest one should be. But she is likely to know the value of speech and a diversity of opinion in a way that non-members don't. She'll have a strong motive and, if we do our work well, a well-developed capacity to distinguish between frauds and potential teachers. In the marketplace of ideas, she'll be a smart shopper. If she hesitates before adopting conventional wisdom on free speech, whether it comes from the left, the right, or the middle, so much the better.

We don't know our students as well as we'd like. But I take comfort in those students from Harvard, whom we met in chapter 1, the ones who, with no particular ideological motive, chided administrators for neglecting the university's mission. I take comfort in Earl Shorris's students debating logic in the wind and cold. And I take comfort in my own students who have shown themselves, everywhere I've been, capable of taking important ideas seriously, even when those ideas seem far, at first, from their immediate concerns, and strange. From early in my career, I've taught Plato to undergraduates. In the beginning, I feared that the only reason I'd been drawn to Plato was that I had uncannily good teachers, which I did. Nonetheless, I found that a few of my own students, much as Earl Shorris's students did, began a love affair with Socrates. More important, even those whose attitude is best characterized as bemused tolerance could be drawn into the work of trying to make better sense than they had been able to make up until then of justice and the good life. I know what Mark Edmundson means when he writes about "finer artistic spirits . . . still alive somewhere in the ether" who might help him out.

We don't necessarily require students who respond to Plato for our case that students are interested in and capable of becoming reasonable people. They can have more prosaic concerns and interests and still be part of what Mill called an "intellectually active people."[64] But that our students can respond to Plato suggests that there is no shortage of interest or capacity in our students for the work of reasoning.

CHAPTER FIVE

The Boycott, Divestment, and Sanctions Movement

A CASE STUDY

Students are capable of becoming reasonable people, but that's not always what their professors want from them.

Imagine that, for a class assignment, you drew a story from a biased source, then massaged the story to render it more biased. Now imagine that your professor, instead of correcting your error, proudly added her name to your essay.

Multiply that one professor by thirty-four, and that's what happened at New York University late in 2018.

There, activists rallied around a resolution against corporations allegedly complicit in Israel's mistreatment of Palestinians. NYU should "divest all capital investments from said corporations." The resolution's authors gestured at "human rights globally" but had eyes only for Israel, which they likened to apartheid-era South Africa.[1]

The charges against Israel included this one: "the IDF [Israel Defense Forces] killed Muhammad al-Faqih in 2016 after he refused to leave his home that was set for demolition." A footnote directs us to *The Electronic Intifada*, whose slant may be deduced from that of its editor, Ali Abunimah. The prior year, after an Israeli couple, residents of a West Bank settlement, were murdered by terrorists as their children looked on, Abunimah tweeted, "Two Israeli settlers killed in West Bank clash."[2]

Yet even Abunimah, in the article the resolution cites, wasn't brazen enough to cast al-Faqih as some civil rights protester, sitting in against home demolitions. He reported, albeit skeptically, that al-Faqih was wanted for murder, and that, according to the IDF, al-Faqih fired at Israeli soldiers.[3] *Haaretz*, a left-of-center paper, headlined its story, "Palestinian Who Murdered Rabbi Michael Mark Killed in West Bank Clashes, Shin Bet Confirms."[4]

"The IDF killed Muhammad al-Faqih in 2016 after he refused to leave his home that was set for demolition" is propaganda. A minute with Google and you know.

Yet thirty-four New York University professors signed on to the resolution, along with fifty-three NYU student organizations. NYU's student government passed it. The vote wasn't close.

I've argued that universities should shape communities whose members take pride in following the evidence and arguments where they lead and share at least provisional standards for evaluating them. When students and professors unite, instead, in spreading propaganda, that should be shocking. Unfortunately, that's just an ordinary day in the campus activities of the Boycott, Divestment, and Sanctions movement (BDS).[5]

I'll now consider the BDS movement in some detail.[6] That's not because it's the most important obstacle to shaping communities of reasonable people on campus. In chapter 2, I've dealt more generally with efforts to shape quite different kinds of communities, whose standards of praise and blame are suited to generating political results. Of these efforts, BDS is just one. But thinking through that case with care will help us see more

concretely than we have so far how a certain way of being political undermines the aim of liberal education I've defended.
Since I've been involved in the fight against BDS, I'm also in a
position to speak to how those who lament anti-Israelism at
universities can combat it without worsening the politicization
they say they hate.

What Is BDS?

Recently, my college, Ursinus College, hosted a discussion of
Israel, during which the Boycott, Divestment, and Sanctions
movement came up. Because the panelists breathe and eat
Israel-related issues, they simply referred to "BDS."

One audience member turned to another and asked, "What's
BDSM?"

I'll explain BDS. If you need help with BDSM, you're on
your own.

In September 2001, the Non-Governmental Organization
Forum, meeting alongside the UN World Conference Against
Racism, urged "complete and total isolation" of Israel, a "racist,
apartheid state," guilty of "acts of genocide."[7] The following
year, activists on American and European campuses demanded
that universities purge their portfolios of companies soiled by
association with Israel. A joint Harvard-MIT divestment peti-
tion attracted more than a hundred faculty signatures. A
counter-petition attracted many more, but the struggle to declare Israel untouchable was on.[8] In the *New York Times*, Matthew Purdy, noting the prevalence of the apartheid charge in
the 2002 debates, observed that the "Israeli-Palestinian conflict
[had] become a struggle-in-residence on college campuses."[9] I
mention the apartheid element because even then, the struggle
was over shunning, not merely criticizing, Israel.

So ostracizing Israel was already in the air when, in 2005, a "Palestinian Civil Society Call for BDS" inaugurated the Boycott, Divestment, and Sanctions movement. The call asks "people of conscience" everywhere "to impose broad boycotts and implement divestment initiatives against Israel similar to those applied to South Africa in the apartheid era." Israel can escape the sanctions only if it ends its "occupation and colonization of all Arab lands," dismantles the security barrier between Israel and the West Bank, recognizes that Arab Palestinians must enjoy "full equality," and protects the right of Palestinian refugees to return to their homes.[10]

I note, although it won't be my focus, that every plank of this call suggests not only an end to Israel's presence in disputed territories, particularly the West Bank, but also the end of Israel as a refuge for or nation of the Jewish people. Sunaina Maira, a professor of Asian American Studies at the University of California, Davis, and a key figure in the movement to isolate Israeli universities, calls BDS an "anti-Zionist and decolonial paradigm."[11] That means Zionism, the project to establish a Jewish state in the Middle East, rather than any particular Israeli misdeed, is what needs undoing. From an anti-Zionist perspective, Israel, "settler-colonial" from the start, has always occupied Arab land.

The "Arab lands" Israel must stop occupying include Israel.

As for the other planks, "full equality" of Israeli-Palestinian citizens is incompatible with any preference for Jews, including Israel's Law of Return, which gives Jews the right to immigrate to Israel. BDS activists consider the Law of Return "racist."[12] And the return of Palestinian refugees—there are more than five million—would, as the journalist, Yair Rosenberg, says, "abrogate" Israel's Jewish character.[13]

I'll focus on Maira because she provides the most extensive insider's account of BDS as it bears on universities. In describing the boycott movement as anti-Zionist and decolonial, she's upfront that BDS aims to redeem the world from the original sin of the establishment of Israel. The BDS call was less forthrightly radical, she says, for "strategic reasons." Perhaps many of those who answer the BDS call believe that Israel is legitimate within its pre-1967 borders, not realizing that "in its de facto application," BDS is "a radical vision of emancipation" that has no room for a Jewish state in the Middle East.[14] As Maira's ally in the boycott movement, Steven Salaita, explains, to be against Zionism is to be against "the notion, in whatever form, that Israel should exist as a Jewish nation-state culturally and demographically, an entity to which Jews anywhere in the world have access." The "Zionist colonization of Palestine started" the Israeli-Palestinian conflict. "Only the decolonization of Palestine will end it."[15]

On the academic scene, the Boycott, Divestment, and Sanctions movement does plenty. Since 2005, student organizations, such as Students for Justice in Palestine (SJP), and sympathetic faculty members have put on Israeli Apartheid Week, a series of events, including lectures, rallies, and performances, meant to justify the pariah status they think Israel deserves. Year after year, campuses witness the strange spectacle of student government representatives, most of whom know little about the Middle East, debating resolutions to divest from Israel or explicitly back the BDS movement. Since 2013, scholarly groups, like the Association for Asian American Studies, the National Association for Chicana and Chicano Studies, and the American Studies Association have stepped outside of their areas of expertise and voted to support the boycott of Israel.[16] Other, bigger, organizations, like the Modern Language Association, have been urged to do so.

In 2019, at Williams College, the student government refused to recognize a club because it's pro-Israel.[17] At Pitzer College, the College Council, which includes faculty, students, and staff, voted to end Pitzer's study abroad program in Haifa.[18] At the University of Illinois, the student senate condemned the view that anti-Zionism is anti-Semitism. The 29–4 vote was taken after hundreds of protesting Jewish students, joined by the lone Jewish senator, walked out. Evidently, few thought it presumptuous for non-Jews, whose knowledge of anti-Semitism, if the resolution is any indication, was derived from the Oxford English Dictionary, to declare which ways of thinking about anti-Semitism are out of order.[19] At the University of California, Berkeley, at a student government meeting, Jewish concerns about representation were dismissed as "Zionist tears," even though the concerned students had said nothing about Israel. After the meeting, some of those students were reportedly told "that being friends with Zionists means one is complicit in oppression, the prison-industrial complex, and modern-day slavery." Perhaps that explains why someone at the meeting, according to a letter signed by twelve Berkeley-based Jewish organizations, shouted "Fuck Zionists!"[20]

We've grown accustomed to these incidents, which occur with depressing frequency, relieved that administrations and boards of trustees, including those at every institution named in the previous paragraph, have refused to go along with BDS. Still, the campaign against Israel is part of the landscape on many campuses. No nation, no matter what its behavior, is similarly targeted.

So What? BDS and Becoming Reasonable People

But I became interested in the Boycott, Divestment, and Sanctions movement less out of concern for Israel than out of concern for higher education.

I first noticed BDS when, in 2013, it was the center of a controversy at Brooklyn College. The College's Students for Justice in Palestine chapter had invited Omar Barghouti, a founder of BDS, and Judith Butler, one of the movement's star professors, to lecture on "the importance of BDS in helping END Israeli apartheid."[21] Co-sponsors consisted mainly of activist groups, including Existence is Resistance and New York City Labor Against the War. But one of the sponsors was not like the others, namely, Brooklyn College's Department of Political Science.

As SJP's advertising made clear, the department wasn't sponsoring, as it would later assert, "a forum for discussion and debate," or as Brooklyn College's president Karen Gould put it, a "forum to discuss important topics" in a "spirit of inquiry." The BDS-friendly controversialist Glenn Greenwald, though he neglected the recruitment piece of the event, came closer to the truth when he asked, "Why shouldn't advocates of a movement be able to gather" to "debate tactics?" In her lecture, Butler admitted that before her and Barghouti's appearance became the talk of the town, she had expected a "conversation with a few dozen student activists."[22]

In a tweet, Corey Robin, a member of the political science department and a BDS activist, wondered what the fuss was about. "We just fucking co-sponsored it," opined he.[23] But sponsorship means, at least, "Check this out." It was fair to question the judgment of Robin and his colleagues. As I argued in chapter 2, political partisanship sits uneasily with the university's efforts to cultivate reason. That doesn't mean that educators should turn away speakers who hope to win their students to a cause. But they have to consider how best to use the speaker, who aims at conversion, to help the university, which aims at reflection. It's not enough, as the department claimed it did, to sponsor all comers. As I argued in chapter 4, merely leading one's students into the presence of opposing zealots isn't teaching. The incident at Brooklyn College was an opportunity to ask about the relationship between BDS, whose presence on campuses was then growing, and the aim President Gould identified as central to the college, open inquiry. What should a college seeking to prepare students for such inquiry do with BDS?

Alas, if people were asking that question, they were drowned out by certain opponents of BDS, like Lewis A. Fidler, then Assistant Leader of the New York City Council. Nine other council members joined Fidler in a letter to President Gould that called for the Butler-Barghouti event to be canceled. It read, in part, "We believe in the principle of academic freedom. However, we also believe in the principle of not supporting schools whose programs we, and our constituents, find to be odious and wrong." After all, a "significant portion of the funding for CUNY schools comes directly from the tax dollars" of New Yorkers.[24]

Nice public funding you have there. It'd be a shame if anything were to happen to it. But we value academic freedom.

Thus, the battle over BDS at Brooklyn College became a rout, pitting heavy-handed, heavy-breathing politicians against doughty defenders of academic freedom. Mayor Michael Bloomberg spoke for many when he said, "If you want to go to a university where the government decides what kind of subjects are fit for discussion, I suggest you apply to a school in North Korea."[25] Game, set, match. Butler and Barghouti spoke the next day. As a final twist, one of the event's lead organizers thanked the freedom warriors who had saved his event by having four pro-Israel students ejected from it.

He feared they might try to distribute flyers.[26]

Lost in all the lobbying was any consideration of what BDS seeks to do in the academy and how best to respond to it, not from a political standpoint, where counterpropaganda may be a necessary response to propaganda, but from an educational standpoint. The case of BDS helps us see in the flesh one attempt to turn colleges and universities into a base—recall the Port Huron Statement—for an "assault on the loci of power." It also helps us think about how colleges or universities, and people who care about them, can respond without compromising the mission of shaping reasonable people. I'll begin by considering the aims and consequences of BDS in an academic setting.

BDS Means War

The Port Huron Statement envisioned "an alliance of students and faculty" with "labor, civil rights, and other liberal forces outside the campus" to transform a radically defective nation. On Maira's account, boycott activism is similarly "embedded" in a movement "that involves progressive left academics, students, union organizers, indigenous activists, human rights advocates, Black radicals" and others.[27] Academic BDS, like the academic left of Port Huron, is self-consciously linked to a wider political movement.

That movement's objectives go beyond booting Israel from the family of nations. The "politics of refusal" of Israel is "part of larger efforts by scholars to transform the university into a site of struggle against militarization as well as racial and class oppression and to challenge US imperial power and its proxies."[28] If that's not transforming the university into a base for an assault on the loci of power, nothing is. One locus, on which BDS focuses nearly all its energy, is Israel. Another is the United States.

The power BDS advocates struggle against is notable not only for its magnitude but also for its wickedness. In 2006,

Maira edited a special issue of the *Journal of Asian American Studies*, which aimed to draw Asian Americanists and Arab Americanists together, in response to certain "political impera-tives."[29] This issue prepared the ground for the Association for Asian American Studies, an otherwise unlikely Middle East policy forum, to adopt BDS seven years later. One contributor, Ibrahim Aoude, a professor of ethnic studies at the University of Hawaii, Manoa, explains the political imperatives in ques-tion. Asian and Arab Americans alike are victims of a United States governed by "fascist ideology and public policy," im-posed to protect "global capitalist development."[30] Maira speaks of "policies of repression, co-optation and domination," prac-ticed in the "everyday state of emergency of US empire."[31] It's not only against Israel but also against the mighty and cruel US empire that the plucky Boycott, Divestment, and Sanctions movement aims its slingshot. If Israel is the sole direct object of BDS, that's presumably because Robin is easier to take down than Batman.

I titled this section "BDS Means War" to highlight Maira's terminology. The "boycott movement is waging a Gramscian war of position, not just a war of maneuver." "Gramscian" refers to the Marxist theorist, Antonio Gramsci, who, Maira explains, "conceptualized the war of position, or cultural and intellectual struggle, in contrast to the war of maneuver, or direct war and open insurrection."[32] Empires like the United States, working through civil society institutions like churches and schools, im-pose on subjects ideas that make them want to kiss their chains. For example, Karl Marx himself argues that what we're told are universal rights are really the rights of "egoistic man, of man separated from other men and from the community."[33] That idea serves property owners well. When the dispossessed start talking redistribution, capitalists yell about the "abolition of individuality and freedom!" They mean, Marx says, "bourgeois individuality" and "bourgeois freedom," the individuality and freedom the ruling class endorses.[34] But it's hard to persuade people who have been raised on "self-evident truths" of that. Until a long war of position dislodges "dominant cultural beliefs," like the belief in individual rights, and establishes a new set of beliefs, or "counter-hegemony," it will be nearly impossible to bring down imperial powers like the United States and Israel.[35]

Maira and her colleagues wage war, too, against the universities that shelter them. "All US universities," Maira argues, "are located within a settler society and are thus settler universities." Just as Israel rose on Arab land, the United States rose on Native American land. Universities in the United States are among the civil society institutions through which the "power of the settler state is upheld." At universities, "US imperial policies are often legitimized, overtly or covertly, through expert knowledge production" and the "repression of resistant knowledges."[36] So BDS struggles against universities as we know them. When practiced by scholars, it's "resistance from within."[37]

When we ask, then, what higher education should do with BDS, we're asking what universities should do with a movement that regards them as part of an "academic-military-prison-industrial complex," against which it is at war.[38]

All's Fair in War: Strategic Ambiguity and Exaggeration

It's hard, I've argued, to make room for reason in politics. That goes double for wars, including wars of position. Even within the academy, BDS supporters try to get people who have almost no knowledge of or stake in learning about the Middle East to adopt controversial propositions about it. They might, like activists in the Modern Language Association, be trying to persuade Shakespeare scholars to boycott Israel. They might, like activists at some colleges, be trying to get a whole student body to support a boycott. They're dealing with what political analysts call low-information voters. Moreover, they believe that they're battling a powerful and pitiless opponent, whose injustices constitute an emergency. No more than generals can they afford to observe the rules that scholars are expected to observe in their fields, or that students are asked to observe in their papers. And they don't. The NYU incident with which I opened is wholly in character. When you think you're in a state of emergency, high-flown talk of becoming reasonable people is a distraction, or perhaps the oppressor's disguise.

As we saw in chapter 3, one standard that professors and students can invoke when reasonable people disagree is clarity. Although there are exceptions, the rule is that members of an intellectual community should present their arguments clearly for evaluation. Arguers shouldn't hide their premises or conclusions. But as we've just seen, Maira acknowledges that BDS sometimes conceals its anti-Zionistic premises for "strategic reasons." This strategic ambiguity reaps dividends. Consider National Public Radio's description of Omar Barghouti, whom you'll remember from the Brooklyn College episode. Barghouti, NPR says, co-founded a movement that "urges boycott, divestment, and sanctions to pressure Israel on security and settlement policies in the West Bank."[39] Perhaps even the drafters of the Palestinian Civil Society Call for BDS dared not dream that, someday, sophisticated journalists would let them pass for mere critics of Israel's West Bank activities. But NPR is hardly alone in doing so.

There's nothing shocking about the use of strategic ambiguity, which politicians practice to draw in more voters than they otherwise could. But colleges and universities that seek to shape reasonable people should be troubled when scholars and students deploy this politician's strategy.

Here's another example of how BDS activists use strategic ambiguity. They describe their movement as "nonviolent," which conjures images of Martin Luther King, Gandhi, and other huggable historical figures. Corey Robin, for example, says that Palestinians "have taken up BDS as a non-violent tactic, precisely the sort of thing that liberal-minded critics have been calling upon them to do for years (where is the Palestinian Gandhi and all that)."[40]

Boycott is a nonviolent tactic. But the BDS movement has no beef with violent tactics. Maira explains that a "war of position" can "lead to, or accompany, a militarized struggle and continue after it."[41]

This ambiguity isn't merely abstract. In October 2015, amid a series of stabbing attacks on Israeli soldiers and civilians, the Palestinian BDS National Committee, the "coordinating body for the BDS campaign worldwide," issued a statement.[42] Whether "the current phase of Israel's intensified repression and Palestinian popular resistance will evolve into a full-fledged intifada or not," it reads, Palestinians are "rising up *en masse* against Israel's brutal, decades-old regime of occupation, settler colonialism, and apartheid."[43] The US Campaign for the Academic and Cultural Boycott of Israel, in whose Organizing Collective Maira serves, issued its own statement, calling for "solidarity with Palestinian resistance."[44]

Neither statement mentions the widely publicized, contemporaneous, stabbing attacks, and there were also nonviolent demonstrations going on at the time. That's the ambiguity. But when you issue a statement in support of resistance in the middle of a "knife intifada," people get the hint. That's not the only one. The first signatory of the 2005 BDS call is the Council of National and Islamic Forces in Palestine, an umbrella group that includes Hamas, Islamic Jihad, and the Popular Front for the Liberation of Palestine, all of which practice and preach violence and all of which have attacked civilians.[45] No doubt some BDS activists have a principled commitment to nonviolence. But BDS as a whole is no more committed to nonviolence than is an army that drops leaflets while it weighs an assault.

Again, there's nothing shocking about strategic ambiguity. Politicians present themselves to different audiences in different ways, and in an America still nostalgic for the civil rights movement, nonviolence sells. But colleges want to teach their students to resist being manipulated, whereas BDS activists want to manipulate them. This is one way in which BDS and the university are at odds.

BDS activists also engage in strategic exaggeration. We know that when a demagogue characterizes the opposition as a nearly all-powerful cabal of journalists, professors, globalists, deep staters, and social media magnates, he's rallying his troops. When he pretends that, despite this opposition, he's wildly popular, he's also rallying his troops. He exaggerates the strength of his enemies and his own strength to make his allies feel part of a miracle movement led by a miracle man. Maira, similarly, exaggerates the BDS movement's strength and the strength of its enemies. She exaggerates its strength when she says that a "host of . . . academic associations" are boycotting.[46] As the list maintained by the US Campaign attests, the boycott, when Maira said that, had been adopted by relatively few, mostly small, academic associations, the most mainstream of which, the American Studies Association, had a reputation for radicalism long before it crashed the Israel-Palestinian conflict.[47] When Maira speaks of a "mass movement supporting BDS in the academy," she exaggerates in the manner of a campaign spokesperson.[48]

She also exaggerates the power of the Zionist enemy, which had supposedly, right up until 2009, when the US Campaign launched, maintained a "lockdown on criticism of Israel in the academy."[49] As we've already seen, the Israeli-Palestinian conflict could be characterized as the struggle-in-residence on college campuses in 2002. The sociologist Amitai Etzioni, who criticizes both sides of that "vicious debate," nonetheless observes that "pro-Israel demonstrators at San Francisco State University [had been] surrounded by people who harassed them with chants like 'Hitler didn't finish the job.'"[50]

They must not have heard about the lockdown on criticism of Israel.

Also in 2002, in the run-up to the Iraq War, more than eight hundred US academics signed a letter warning that Israel might be planning to use the fog of war to perpetrate "full-fledged ethnic cleansing."[51] Neither the fifty-three University of California, Berkeley professors who signed, nor the twenty-nine New York University professors who signed, nor the eighteen Harvard professors who signed, nor the seven hundred or so other professors who signed had heard about the lockdown. Joel Beinin, then president of the Middle East Studies Association (MESA), whose views on Israel were well known prior to his elevation to that position, was a signatory. Laurie Brand, who would serve as president of MESA in 2004, was also a signatory. So was Fred Donner, who went on to serve as president in 2012 and had been a board member in the early 1990s.[52] Even the discipline of Middle East Studies hadn't caught wind of the lockdown.[53]

That's because there has never been a lockdown on criticism of Israel. It's true that scholars who question Israel's right to exist can face scrutiny and blowback. If you draw additional attention by tweeting that a Jewish journalist's "story should have ended at the pointy end of a shiv," you may find your career derailed, as did Steven Salaita. Salaita had also tweeted, amid fears, later confirmed, that kidnapped young Israelis had been killed, "I wish all the fucking West Bank settlers would go missing."[54] I don't think that the University of Illinois should have canceled Salaita's hire, but their action hardly qualifies as suppressing "Israel criticism." Often, when someone in BDS complains about being silenced, they do it from behind a podium at a college or university. About their silencing, they can't say enough.

As for Maira herself, who assembles an "archive of repression" and speaks of the "censorship" of boycott advocates, her book was published by the prestigious University of California Press. It's part of a series edited by Lisa Duggan and Curtis Marez, both BDS advocates and both, with Maira, members of the American Studies Association Executive Council that pushed the 2013 boycott through.[55]

Worst lockdown ever.

Maira's exaggeration of Zionist power is more serious than exaggerations of BDS success for two reasons. First, it encourages students and scholars falsely to believe that a "collusion of Zionism and neoliberalism" explains much that goes on at universities. Maira quotes, with approval, two scholars who argue that the plight of academic labor is connected to "Zionist interventions in the academy," and that one must, therefore, "de-

Zionize" higher education.[56] The reasoning of Maira's scholars runs something like this:

1. Once, the University of Illinois fired Steven Salaita.
2. Its Chancellor served on the board of Nike.
3. Nike sells shoes in Israel.
4. One of Nike's suppliers operates in a settlement.
5. So Nike is de facto Zionist. It's also a corporation. So corporations and Zionists are on the same page.
6. That means that collusion between Zionists and corporate interests did Salaita in.
7. Therefore, "university policymakers consort with corporate profiteers," who consort with Zionists, in all universities.
8. So "the solution is to 'de-Zionize' our campuses."

I wish I were kidding. Look for yourself.[57]

This kind of conspiracy-minded thinking is more damaging than cheerleading exaggerations. It represents a whole, sloppy, mode of reasoning, rather than isolated misstatements.

The second reason, I won't dwell on, because it's not at the heart of this book's concerns. But when you hook Zionism to the rule of moneyed interests and suggest that its defeat would cure many seemingly unrelated ills, you activate dangerous, anti-Semitic ideas. In recent years, Jewish Voice for Peace, a pro-BDS organization active on campuses, has been running a campaign called Deadly Exchange, which targets US law enforcement trips to Israel. These trips, they say, some of which are sponsored by "Jewish organizations," "promote and extend . . . extrajudicial executions . . . police murders . . . and attacks on human rights defenders." Thus, this story goes, do Jewish organizations, out of slavish devotion to Israel, sell out "immigrants and refugees, as well as all people of color, Muslims, trans and queer people."⁵⁸ I get it. If you pin absolutely everything on the Zionists, you win more allies than you otherwise could. But you're swimming in pretty fetid water.

Lockstep

When it comes to BDS, there's no lockdown, but there is a lockstep, a marching in close order that helps armies but hinders universities that seek to shape reasonable people.

The first academic association in America to adopt BDS was the Association for Asian American Studies, whose acquaintance we made earlier in the chapter.⁵⁹

Its resolution to adopt BDS rested on a number of controversial propositions.

It rested on the proposition that Asian American Studies scholars ought to be speaking, as scholars, about the Middle East or, as they put it, "West Asia."

It rested on the proposition that Israel has committed crimes grave enough to warrant boycott and that Israeli universities are complicit enough in those crimes to be targeted.

It rested on the proposition that BDS is a moral way of expressing one's misgivings about Israel. You can be, after all, a harsh critic of Israel and object to abolishing it.

It rested on the proposition that BDS is a wise strategy for helping Palestinians, even though Noam Chomsky, the renowned linguist and Israel critic, considers it a "gift to Israeli and US hardliners," who wish to charge their opponents with "pure anti-Semitism." That charge, Chomsky says, can be made against the BDS approach "with justice." In Chomsky's view, because BDS makes such a fat target for those who want to discredit pro-Palestinian work, it's a strategy one might profitably adopt if one "hates the Palestinians."⁶⁰

Reasonable people disagree about such propositions, but within the Association for Asian American Studies, no disagreement is evident. AAAS is not a large organization, but it's a little big for unanimity, particularly among academics, who are nothing if not quarrelsome and contentious. According to the president and executive board at the time, about seven hundred members, presumably a fraction of the full membership, attended the 2013 conference at which the resolution was adopted. And about 10% of the membership attended the general business meeting where the resolution was discussed and voted on. There were no nays. There were no abstentions. Evidently, no one disagreed, even with the anonymity a secret ballot provided, with any of the above propositions.

It's jarring to find scholars unanimous to the extent our scholars of Asian American Studies are. One might expect a discipline to agree on certain fundamental principles, as I imagine biologists agree in broad outline about evolution. But what causes a group of scholars to come forward in total agreement about disputed moral, strategic, and factual matters that fall, for the most part, outside of their areas of expertise? The short answer is the political imperatives Maira and her colleagues had named years before, or the "war of position" Maira would name years later; scholars are known for disagreeing, but soldiers are known for standing shoulder to shoulder.

Still, we were talking only about one business meeting. In an open letter published roughly a month after the resolution came out, I proposed that the complete absence of dissent within AAAS about the resolution was a sign of disciplinary ill health.[61] I appealed to those—I assumed they existed—who had doubts to make those doubts publicly known. I hurried to get the letter out because unanimity was my whole hook, and I didn't think it could last.

I needn't have rushed. It has been seven years, and not one blog post or op-ed has surfaced.[62]

Let me remind you of a claim of Jacques Berlinerblau, which I touched on in chapter 2. The "politicized professor" wishes he "could walk from one side of the campus to another and never find an alternative to his worldview."[63] In its neighborhood of the academy, with respect to BDS, the Association for Asian American Studies is living that dream. The more and bigger such neighborhoods are, the fewer colleges and universities can be communities whose members seek to become reasonable people.

Opposing BDS: Campus Don'ts

So yes, BDS is founded on an ideology that disparages the university's claim to be a home of reason, viewing it instead as an arm of an illegitimate and cruel state. Its scholar supporters see themselves less as members of a university community than as resisters, stationed in the belly of the beast. BDS seeks to sign up students and scholars to Middle East commitments they have neither the time nor the inclination to research. So its activists have to use and encourage others to use the strategic maneuvers that politicians use, only more so, because we're talking not just about an ordinary political campaign, but a war. BDS fosters solidarity at the expense of inquiry. For all these reasons, colleges and universities should be wary of BDS.

But they shouldn't squash it or its ideas. Colleges are used to professors whose ideas contradict their mission statements. We've already seen how a Marxist might think the university's claim to independence is a lie. A Freudian might tell you that seemingly rational disputes among scholars represent the surface of things, whose depths can be sounded only through psychoanalysis. A Rousseauian might tell you that universities are too close to the societies they inhabit to avoid corruption; serious thinkers need solitude and distance.

In the best case, such renegades will do what any university, as I proposed in chapter 2, can expect of anyone entering with an agenda. They'll agree to follow arguments and evidence where they lead. I think of a professor the authors of *Passing on the Right* mention, a Marxist, who introduced his students to Friedrich Hayek's *The Road to Serfdom*. "I'm going to assign the book I most disagree with in the twentieth century," he told them, and asked that they "recreate its arguments with intellectual empathy."[64] He gained for Hayek, a hero to many conservatives, at least one convert, and who knows how many students were introduced to Hayek's thought in this manner?

Even when professors don't respect the mission of the university, so long as they don't abuse their positions to advance their aims, a university needn't sweat a few self-styled revolutionaries. That a handful of professors guzzle the university's sherry as they plot to gain control of it is a price a university can afford to pay for a strong challenge to its own premises which, after a while, are nearly as likely to be accepted without question as are the premises of other kinds of institutions. Communities of inquiry should be distinguished by their reluctance to shut down even obnoxious and radical challengers.

To be sure, when people wage war with you, you want to wage war right back. When I have my pro-Israel hat on, outside of the college setting, I try to win the argument, even to demoralize my anti-Israel opponents. In a college setting, one should, when confronted with a challenging argument, confront it where it's strongest. Outside of that setting, one is sometimes content to hit an argument where it's weakest and let the opposition take care of itself. Because I think that the restraints teachers and scholars observe have value outside of colleges, I don't go nearly as far as other sedentary keyboard combatants do in playing to win. But in political conflicts, he who doesn't try to win risks coming to ruin among those who do.

So I don't blame people, particularly those outside the university, for wanting to meet BDS propaganda with anti-BDS counterpropaganda, ardent and eloquent anti-Zionists with ardent and eloquent Zionists, fire with fire.[65] But those who look after the well-being of colleges and universities will avoid strategies that undermine them almost as surely as the BDS movement does.

Here's one strategy best avoided. If you care about universities, don't practice viewpoint discrimination. In 2017, Fordham University's administration refused club status to Students for Justice in Palestine. The refusal occurred after Dean of Students Keith Eldredge asked student organizers a series of questions about their beliefs—for example, "Why use the term apartheid" to describe Israel? Eldredge decided that he couldn't greenlight an organization "whose sole purpose is advocating political goals of a specific group, and against a specific country." That would be "contrary to the mission and values of the University."[66]

If Fordham were a public university, bound by the First Amendment, this would be an easy case. In *Healy v. James* (1972), the Supreme Court ruled on a similar matter, Central Connecticut State's denial of club status to Students for a Democratic Society, the group, incidentally, behind the Port Huron Statement. The Court said, the "College, acting here as the instrumentality of the State, may not restrict speech or association simply because it finds the views expressed by any group to be abhorrent."[67] Moreover, to justify restrictions, it wouldn't be enough that a group's philosophy set it at odds with campus regulations. A college can demand that a club agree to abide by such regulations. It cannot demand that a club agree that such regulations are good. So, although SJP nationally has favored the tactic of disrupting speakers, a tactic that often runs afoul of student conduct codes, Fordham couldn't, if it were a state university, reject the club on those grounds alone.

Fordham has already lost one state court battle in this matter on the grounds that it reneged on its own contractually binding promises to protect freedom of expression.[68] But the Court that decided *Healy v. James* explained, picking up language from a previous case, why universities should make such promises in the first place: "The college classroom, with its surrounding environs, is peculiarly the 'marketplace of ideas.'"[69] That implies that colleges, with the exception of those dedicated to spreading religious or other creeds, should have more, not fewer, safeguards for freedom of inquiry than other institutions have. For those who—to return to Locke's language—"see but in part" and "know but in part," such freedom is a necessary condition of becoming reasonable.[70] Universities have years and a multitude of resources at their disposal to initiate students into the charms and uses of being reasonable and of belonging to a community of reasonable people. If we can't, without suppressing viewpoints, compete with propagandists, we may as well fold our tents.

There's another, related, strategy, university people can't condone: attacking our students. Agreed, terror organizations, through the Council of National and Islamic Forces in Palestine, endorsed the BDS call. Agreed, the BDS movement plays with anti-Semitic fire. But it's a long way from there to putting the names and sometimes the faces of students on posters proclaiming them terror supporters or Jew-haters because they're involved in pro-BDS organizations. David Horowitz's Freedom Center has done just this on several campuses.[71]

Horowitz has drawn on a site called Canary Mission, whose purpose is explained in a promotional video.[72] "It is your duty," the narrator says, to "ensure that today's radicals are not tomorrow's employees." On occasion, Canary Mission does a service— if I were Lara Kollab's potential employer or patient, I'd want to know that she tweeted, not so long ago, that she would "purposely give all the yahood [Jews] the wrong meds."[73] Canary Mission deserves credit for exposing instances of extreme anti-Semitism. But the organization casts a much wider net than that. For example, it profiles five of the students involved in attempting to start a Students for Justice in Palestine chapter at Fordham. Most have done little more than that to attract Canary Mission's attention. In one case, the sole additional dirt Canary Mission could shovel on a student was that she had once retweeted a pro-BDS article. For that, a college sophomore should have her picture shared nationally in an effort to deny her a job?[74]

That's shameful. And anyone looking to make inroads into universities ought to know that professors don't take kindly to attempts to harm their students. I've come across a few anti-Zionist students. Some of them might have joined a BDS organization if one happened to exist on my campus, but every one of them was also thoughtful, well-meaning, and entirely undeserving of the treatment Canary Mission dishes out to the students they catch. In the debate over Israel on campus, it's important to draw attention to the implicit and explicit anti-Semitism that crops up around the BDS movement. But the mission of universities is to educate, not destroy students, and so those who care about universities will do the work of exposing anti-Semitism in such a way as to do as little harm to students as possible.

As I've said, outside of a scholarly setting, I have no quarrel with engaging in something like a political campaign against BDS. They've got their campaign, and we need ours. Without drawing any equivalence between BDS and its opponents, I concede that campaigns are rarely scholarly and nearly always unfair. But contrary to one defender of Canary Mission, I can't agree that scruples are a sign of weakness, "morally admirable," but "not always martially effective."[75] Even outside the university, BDS isn't a fight that requires us to sacrifice our young. Inside the university, I think I speak for most professors, including the pro-Israel ones, when I say that, rare cases aside, when you go after my students, I'm inclined to go after you.

Opposing BDS: Campus Dos

It's naïve to imagine that good ideas drive out bad ideas in most communities. Defenders of freedom of speech usually limit themselves to arguing that the free exchange of ideas, when you weigh the benefits and costs, offers the best prospect for driving out bad ideas.

The prospect is still better for a community of reasonable people, with a shared pride in being guided by the best evidence and arguments, some shared standards for judging arguments, and experience in the use of those standards.

It's naïve to imagine that the universities and scholarly associations BDS targets are communities of reasonable people. But the aspiration to be reasonable persists in them. The way one opposes BDS should honor that aspiration.

It just might work. In January 2016, a group called Historians Against the War (HAW), which had previously endorsed boycotting Israel, asked the American Historical Association to commit itself to "monitoring Israeli actions restricting the right to education in the Occupied Palestinian Territories."[76] This wasn't a boycott resolution, but since it was put forward by a pro-BDS faction, it was regarded as a test of BDS strength. And, as the University of Maryland, College Park historian, Jeffrey Herf, put it, the resolution's "whereas" clauses amounted to "an indictment of the policies of the government of Israel towards Palestinian universities in the West Bank and Gaza," policies frequently invoked to justify a boycott.[77]

Herf and others opposed to the resolution appealed to the professional consciences of their colleagues, most of whom probably had no rooting interest one way or another. Partly, they disputed how Historians Against the War interpreted evidence. For example, as a summary of arguments prepared by some of the scholars opposing the resolution said, the HAW's own "footnoted evidence [did] not support one sweeping claim, that the Israeli 'military routinely invades campuses.'" Historians, they argued, "should not present one-sided narratives as 'fact' and must remain sensitive to the range of perspectives on contested events." Partly, where they were willing to concede a fact, they took HAW to task for neglecting "relevant context." Yes, the Israeli army had attacked the Islamic University of Gaza. But "Hamas used the Islamic University to build, test, and possibly launch rockets."[78] Herf and his allies didn't demand that their fellow historians accept Israel's explanations of its actions. Instead, they argued that historians should "acknowledge the limits of [their] ability *as* historians," whose subject matter isn't usually ripped from the headlines, "to reach a judgment about the facts in dispute."[79]

At the American Historical Association's business meeting, the resolution failed, with 51 ayes and 111 nays.

The professional standards of historians aren't identical to the standards, including clarity, comprehensiveness, and depth, that guide us when reasonable people disagree. But in urging their colleagues not to form a judgment that went beyond what the evidence could support, the resolution's opponents were asking their colleagues to be reasonable.

One can't be sure whether that way of framing the debate was what won the day. But Herf, reflecting on an earlier battle, concludes that his colleagues can be swayed by the appeal to professionalism which, in the case of historians, is also an appeal to reason. People wrote him after that earlier battle, "expressing their opposition to various Israeli policies," and in some cases, their view that "Israel is a nationalist anachronism." But they sided with Herf. Herf thinks "that the decisive factor was their self-respect *as scholars.*"[80] What one can say for sure is that this mode of opposing BDS is perfectly in tune with the well-being of colleges and universities.

Outside our professional associations and inside our colleges and universities we might try what many of us do best, namely, teaching. In "Loud and Fast versus Slow and Quiet: Responses to Anti-Israel Activism on Campus," Jeffrey Kopstein, my fellow political scientist, writes about his time as director of the Centre for Jewish Studies at the University of Toronto. Kopstein has no illusions about "campus organizations hostile to Israel," which he considers "less interested in criticizing Israeli policy than in effacing and deleting its existence." Still, he resisted calls to counter anti-Israel activity with pro-Israel activity, judging that it often resulted less in "countering speech with speech" than in "screaming against screaming." This screaming not only does the university no good but also does Israel's reputation no good. Most "students and faculty members have scattered knowledge of the history and complexities of the region" and will, therefore, take the "cognitive shortcut of identifying with the 'out group,'" which at least in left-liberal neighborhoods is more often than not going to be the Palestinians.[81]

Judging, too, that "the strong point of universities is teaching and research," that "professors are not activists," and that "politicizing the classroom is what we want to avoid at all costs," Kopstein and his colleagues set about the "slow, quiet, thoughtful and unglamorous work of teaching thousands of students in a range of disciplines" about the "true complexity of the situation." They "cultivated connections with Israeli academic institutions." They taught "dozens and dozens of courses."[82] In so doing, they didn't necessarily shape Zionists; they did shape "a large cohort of students with a deeper knowledge of the [Arab-Israeli] conflict." "Their presence," the presence of people who know propaganda when they see it, can influence "the broader campus in ways that the screaming matches of campus activism do not."[83]

On my own campus, after a rare instance of campus tension concerning Israel, I met with a colleague with whom I'd butted heads. I don't know whether he was an anti-Zionist, but he was a man of the left and had ties to an anti-Zionist organization. We agreed to work together to achieve roughly the aim Kopstein describes, though our small college doesn't have the resources to teach dozens and dozens of courses on the conflict. We arranged a small group discussion of Israeli elections. We managed a reading group on Ari Shavit's then much-talked-about *My Promised Land*. With a colleague in Jewish Studies, we arranged discussions on matters of Jewish social and political interest, including a panel on anti-Semitism. Together, we taught a course on Zionism, whose students included Zionists and those who had serious doubts about Zionism. We crafted a syllabus on the history and philosophy of Zionism in which we tried, in part by not including any text we couldn't convince the other was worth reading, to keep free of political bias. We agreed to try, as an example for our students, to follow the arguments wherever they might lead.

I don't know where students came down on Zionism at the end of the course. But one student, who was, in his own words, "obsessed with the Israeli-Palestinian conflict," had "not been well-read on Zionist history." The course introduced him to "ideas [he] hadn't come across."[84] As important, he and other students in the class, some of whom came in with strong opinions about the Israeli-Palestinian conflict, had the experience of confronting the other side, not through, in Kopstein's terms, "screaming against screaming," but through a semester-long discussion. In the admittedly imperfect way these things happen in classrooms, they were compelled to look at the same evidence together and hold each other's arguments up to scrutiny, in front of other students who had also looked at the evidence. Perhaps students who experience this kind of class will perform the same work as Kopstein supposes his University of Toronto students did. That work isn't to represent the pro-Israel side against the anti-Israel side but to demand, whatever one's leanings may be, something more than propaganda about Israel. Such students might demand, with respect to the Israeli-Palestinian conflict and other matters, to be treated as reasonable people.

Conclusion

FIGHTING FOR MORE OF
THIS, AND LESS OF THAT

As I write, in 2020, conservatives are debating what it means to fight.

Jeffrey Kopstein, whom we just met, isn't a conservative as far as I know. But we can learn from his approach to fighting BDS, which, perhaps more than any other campus movement, is the conservative specter of left indoctrination made solid.

For Kopstein, fighting BDS is a long, teaching game that has, with respect to Zionism, an uncertain outcome. Kopstein and his Toronto colleagues taught dozens of courses. Kopstein thinks they shaped a critical mass of informed students, familiar with "the long and incremental work of intellectual inquiry." Those students, nonetheless, didn't "necessarily become Zionists."[1]

The strategy Kopstein describes is ambitious. It attempts to change how the Israeli-Palestinian conflict is discussed on campus. It attempts to help students become reasonable about an issue that generates a great deal of propaganda and passion. It counts on the students it reaches to influence other students.

But the strategy is also modest: "Anti-Israel propaganda that edges over into antisemitism will probably never go away."[2] If the strategy succeeds, campuses change subtly, not dramatically. Israeli apartheid week and its slanders don't end. But fewer students participate, and fewer students mistake the formulas and dogmatism of the activists for intellectual or moral seriousness.

Campus cultures aren't all one thing. But if we do our work, there will be more of that culture in which it's shameful to commit oneself without weighing the arguments and the evidence, and less of that culture according to which it's shameful to hesitate to commit oneself. In their neighborhood of the university, Kopstein and his colleagues did what I've argued colleges and universities should do: they worked, over a long period, to maintain a climate in which following the arguments and evidence where they lead is praiseworthy and failing to do so is blameworthy.

Broadened beyond the conflict over Israel on campus, that's the right ambitious and modest way to think about the work of those who care about our colleges and universities. It's also the kind of long view that my fellow conservatives, ordinarily proponents of gradual change, should like. But a vocal group of conservatives thinks that we're in crisis, that we're about to lose, permanently, a war for the culture, and that, in this war, colleges are an enemy asset. They think, like the anti-BDS activists out to ruin the employment prospects of pro-BDS students, that we need to fight fire with fire.

Campus is just one front in a wide war. Sohrab Ahmari, a prominent conservative journalist, urges people like me to "fight the culture war with the aim of defeating the enemy and enjoying the spoils in the form of a public square re-ordered to the common good and ultimately the Highest Good."[3] Conservatives are urged to learn politics as "war and enmity." Our progressive enemies know that a "culture war means discrediting their opponents and weakening or destroying their institutions." Conservatives, too many of whom are naïvely attached to "civility and decency," had better learn to "approach the culture war with a similar realism," lest they come to ruin among so many who are not good. Some conservatives are, after all, partisans in the scorched-earth style.

We're already nearly ruined because, according to this argument, liberal political philosophy, from John Locke on, has favored individual freedom over tradition, authority, and a sense of human limits. "Conservative liberals"—like Patrick Deneen, Ahmari takes us to be part of the problem—don't grasp that liberal democracy has always been a hostile environment for conservatives, especially religious believers, and has grown more hostile as its logic has unfolded. To overcome this built-in disadvantage, and to overcome our unscrupulous enemies, conservatives must overcome their own scruples about civility and limited government, and battle to establish "our order." In this, one recognizes the spirit of Michael Anton's "Flight 93 Election," with which this book began.

Ahmari, unlike Anton, doesn't accuse other conservatives of putting paychecks and popularity before principle. But he does, singling out the conservative commentator and legal activist, David French, make them out to be prisses. French is a religious conservative who thinks, nonetheless, that persuasion and, if necessary, appeals to the law within a "classical liberal framework" offer the best means of defending conservative rights and interests.[4] In this respect, French, too, is a conservative liberal. But Ahmari thinks that French's unwillingness to gear up for an all-out war against liberalism represents an "airy, above-it-all mentality."[5] Conservatives like French and me fret about forms and formalities and arguments while our fellow conservatives are being driven from the public square. We need, as they say, a fighter.

With this dispute in mind, let's return to higher education, where French has played a role as president of the Foundation for Individual Rights in Education (FIRE), about which we heard in chapter 4, from 2004 to 2005, and as an attorney defending the First Amendment and due process rights of students and professors. FIRE isn't a conservative group, but it shares with conservatives the worry that students can be subjected to "indoctrination" in "radical political orthodoxies" at universities. Such orthodoxies are among the threats to freedom of speech, religion, and association on campus that FIRE combats.[6]

FIRE fights in courts of law, when rights are directly threatened by a university's policies or officials, and in courts of public opinion, when the threat is not direct. It has prospered in both. French explains that as late as 2009, about 70% of colleges and universities surveyed by FIRE had at least one policy that "clearly restricted constitutionally protected expression." Thanks to a "legal and political onslaught," in which FIRE was prominent, only 28.5% of them today fit that description.[7] Recently, FIRE has campaigned to convince colleges to adopt their own versions of the "Chicago Principles," an endorsement, originating at the University of Chicago, of free speech as essential to the free inquiry for which modern universities stand. As of this writing, seventy higher education institutions, from Princeton University to Gettysburg College to the University of Colorado System, have adopted a version.[8]

I note these victories not to affirm what I've so far denied, namely that the teaching mission of colleges and universities ends once freedom of speech and inquiry are established. Nor do I think that merely adopting the Chicago Principles establishes freedom of speech and inquiry. I note FIRE's successes only to affirm that even at universities, where left-wing activists have more sway than in the country at large, an incremental approach—more of this, less of that—has succeeded beyond what one might have predicted. Those demanding that we fight fire with fire should pay more attention to FIRE.

Roger Kimball, a long-time higher education critic and an ally of Ahmari's, has another idea: "starve Academia Inc. of funds." Recall Ahmari's militant advice: defeating progressives means "discrediting them" and "weakening or destroying their institutions." Kimball, who chairs the William F. Buckley, Jr. Program at Yale University, knows that, along with occasional left-wing protests, Yale features the Directed Studies Program, which gives about a hundred "first-year students an intense interdisciplinary introduction to some of the seminal texts of Western civilization."[9] It's the kind of program to which a conservative might say, "More of this, less of that." But Kimball says, instead, that "most" colleges and universities are "dedicated to the destruction" of the "pursuit of truth" and of "the highest values of our civilization." No doubt Kimball knows he's over the top when, donning his Falwell mask, he urges parents and alumni to "refuse to subsidize [the] perversion" that universities practice.[10] Perhaps Kimball, a cultured man, is embarrassed to find his name attached to an article entitled, "PC Insanity May Mean the End of American Universities." But these are the sacrifices one makes as a realist concerning war and enmity.

Enemies can come to resemble each other. So it's no surprise that some conservatives share the view of their progressive opponents, that colleges and universities, whose dedication to reason is a sham, are instruments of a ruling elite, whose dedication to freedom and equality is a sham. It's no surprise that some conservatives share the view that we should wage war against universities, albeit from without rather than from within. It's no surprise that some conservatives share the view that everything is political, that politics is about dominance and subjection, and that those conservatives who think otherwise are squishes.

But come on.

More precisely, why would a conservative prefer this strategy, which requires us to abandon reason and which has no track record, to French's, which doesn't require us to abandon reason and has an impressive track record?

Let me turn from conservatives to others who take an interest in higher education.

The "American campus," Kopstein says despite his intimate familiarity with the propagandizing that takes place there, "is still a place where intellectual arguments carry weight."[11] It's also a place where reason carries weight. Just not as much as one might wish. I think the overwhelming majority of university people—students, faculty, staff—agree, most of the time, that rational inquiry is fruitful, even honorable. However, not only left-liberal partisanship but also habit, interest, overconfidence, hope, fear, and other human things guarantee that becoming reasonable, even at colleges and universities, requires constant attention. Allan Bloom may have called the university the home of reason,[12] but he didn't imagine that it occupied many rooms. Blink, and someone has locked it in the attic. As we saw in chapter 2, when we considered the many constituencies at the university that "don't want no trouble," there's a whole lot of blinking going on.

I was heartened, however, by the founding, in 2015, of the Heterodox Academy, led by Jonathan Haidt, whom we encountered in chapter 4. Like FIRE, the Heterodox Academy isn't a conservative organization. At last check, their membership was—members classified themselves—16% conservative, 17% progressive, 25% centrist, and 26% libertarian.[13] The Heterodox Academy grew out of concern with the leftward tilt of the field of social psychology. But the concern was not that the tilt was unfair or, as a Kimball might suggest, coming to eat your children. Rather, the concern was that political uniformity "reduces the quality of science published in social psychology." One-sidedness, among other things, makes us more skeptical of some results than of others and narrows our understanding of what questions merit investigation.[14]

As I said in chapter 3, the scientific community, among whom I'd include the kinds of social scientists who are drawn to the Heterodox Academy, cultivates pride in drawing only those conclusions that the best arguments and evidence available permit. The cause of the university is usually taken up by cranky, old-fashioned humanists—I am one—whose power in higher education is negligible. But scientists, even if they need to be convinced that their science-challenged colleagues are also reasoners, are a natural, powerful, and potentially vocal constituency for liberal education understood as the shaping of reasonable people. May the Heterodox Academy attract and inspire many of them.

The Heterodox Academy won't fix higher education any more than Kopstein and company ended BDS at the University of Toronto. American higher education, encompassing for-profits and non-profits, big universities and small colleges, public and private institutions, and serving around 16 million students, is too big and diverse to change in some one way. The Heterodox Academy's particular emphases, on diversity of viewpoint and constructive dialogue, may or may not be the best emphases. The Academy's 4,000 or so members,[15] some more involved than others, will have their work cut out for them trying to make a dent in a higher education system that employs well over a million faculty members. But the Heterodox Academy gives us a sense of what kinds of people, not now much engaged in liberal education, could become engaged in it.

If we define "us" as those inside and outside of universities who think the attempt to become reasonable is worth making at universities, and "them" as those inside and outside universities who consider this attempt naïve or harmful, I think there are more of us than there are of them.

I'm heartened, too, that one doesn't need great numbers to make meaningful progress. Robert George, a social conservative who founded, two decades ago, the James Madison Program in American Ideals and Institutions, says that it "really doesn't take a hundred professors, it takes five to make an enormous difference on campus." George's work is animated by the idea of the university as a "forum for the vibrant, robust discussion of the spectrum of points of view that are held by reasonable, responsible people." He thinks that his program, quite beyond its immediate focus on constitutionalism and political theory, has effected, over time, a "transformation of the ethos" at Princeton in a direction favorable to "true diversity of opinion and the exploration of ideas." No doubt, as George also asserts, the success and longevity of his Princeton program have softened the ground for programs elsewhere, a few of which I referred to in chapter 2, which flourish at both elite and non-elite institutions.[16]

I might be reluctant to take a Kopstein or a George at his word, but the experience they describe is also my own. The Great Ideas major I helped put together at Carthage College, and the Common Intellectual Experience, in which I've taught at Ursinus College, required the support of a majority of the faculty. But they were set in motion by a handful of people—I don't have an exact count, but George's five sounds about right. And I've seen the influence such programs have on campus beyond the individual classrooms in which they're taught. Like Kopstein, and in line, I think, with a conservative approach to change, I'd emphasize that top to bottom transformation and an end to all campus woes aren't in the offing. Amelioration, however, is not only possible but also, if one can look beyond the scary higher education headlines, observable.

We should do much more to observe it. When an undergraduate at Washington University in St. Louis writes a column for the school newspaper entitled "It's Okay That Conservatives Don't Feel Welcome," you may hear about it from conservative publications like the *Daily Wire*, from conservative intellectuals like Rod Dreher, and even from *Fox & Friends*.[17] But if, less than a year later, that same university's entire freshman class is reading and discussing a superb book on free speech, authored by Nadine Strossen, one of its best advocates, you may not hear about *that* at all.[18] Such lopsided coverage, though unsurprising, is a disservice not only to our colleges and universities but also to students and parents trying to make wise decisions about them. I hope this book has done something to redress it, even if one book can't do much. More of this, less of that.

I spent my college and graduate school years at the University of Chicago, so I'll end with a thought inspired by that most famous of Chicago presidents, Robert Maynard Hutchins.

Colleges and universities, particularly those without billion-dollar endowments, have to figure out how to react to constituencies that can help or harm them. They have to consider parents and students who worry about jobs, corporations who want students to arrive fully trained in Excel and computer-assisted widget design, politicians who have diverse and conflicting agendas, alumni and donors who give and refuse gifts, and student activists who may generate unflattering headlines.

No one demands, at least explicitly, that universities organize themselves to shape people who measure themselves by their adherence to reason. Even if I'm right that there are more of us than there are of them, that means only that there are more people who think it's possible and desirable to cultivate reason at universities than there are people who don't. That's something different from clamoring for that mission.

Universities respond to the demands they see in front of them, get pulled in many directions, and seem to stand for everything and nothing. Hutchins, leading and writing amid the Great Depression, was no stranger to external pressures. Nonetheless, speaking particularly of the university's need for money, he said that "when an institution determines to do something in order to get money it must lose its soul, and frequently does not get the money." Universities that make programs to chase cash are "likely to be unbalanced and confused." It's not, he adds, "that universities do not need money" or "that they should not try and get it." Rather, they should "have an educational policy and then try to finance it, instead of letting financial accidents determine their educational policy."[19] Sociologist and Chicago man, Donald Levine, wrote a book about the University of Chicago to address a "shortage of moral and intellectual resources for energizing higher education" that is no less acute now than it was when his book came out in 2006.[20] The history of the University of Chicago could, Levine thought, help in that shortage precisely because Hutchins and others weren't timid. They set out to change the way Americans thought about education, rather than hiring teams of consultants, a new team each year, to figure out, as waiters say, how everything is tasting. That's inspiring, but it's also a rebuke not only to timid administrators but also to faculty members, protected by tenure, who don't want no trouble.

I think and have argued that, even without a great preacher's effort of the sort Hutchins undertook, liberal education understood as the shaping of reasonable people can be made attractive to students of the kind I've taught and to their parents. I agree with Samuel Abrams, who, despite a harrowing run-in with student activists, examines the best survey data we have to find that most students seek "a multiplicity of ideas and experiences" and "take pride in their ability to absorb, confront, engage, and react to these varied views."[21] I agree with Jonathan Haidt and Greg Lukianoff, who think that "market forces" will reward universities that, recognizing many obstacles to rational inquiry and disagreement, establish conditions in which faculty and students can engage well in both.[22] I'm convinced, then, that, for defenders of liberal education, the present is not as bad a time as the shouting of culture warriors and the lectures of consultants might lead us despairingly to believe. Now, perhaps even more than in other times, those who love reason and know its fragility can be persuaded and, in turn, persuade others that liberal education addresses a permanent need.

NOTES

Preface

1. John Locke, *Some Thoughts Concerning Education*, in *Some Thoughts Concerning Education* and *Of the Conduct of the Understanding*, ed. Nathan Tarcov and Ruth Grant (Indianapolis, IN: Hackett, 1996), 141.

2. Leo Strauss, *Liberalism: Ancient and Modern* (Ithaca, NY: Cornell University Press, 1968), ix.

3. George F. Will, *The Conservative Sensibility* (New York: Hachette Books, 2019), xvii, xxix.

4. Jefferson to Henry Lee, May 8, 1825.

5. Jefferson to Roger C. Weightman, June 24, 1826.

6. Will, *Conservative Sensibility*, 20.

7. Will, *Conservative Sensibility*, xxviii.

8. Locke, *Thoughts*, 95. For more on this aspect of Locke, see my "Principle and Practice in Locke's *Some Thoughts Concerning Education*," in Christopher Lynch and Jonathan Marks, eds., *Principle and Prudence in Western Political Thought* (Albany: State University of New York Press, 2016), 133–49.

9. Alexis de Tocqueville, *Democracy in America*, trans. Harvey Mansfield and Delba Winthrop (Chicago: University of Chicago Press, 2000), 12.

10. Locke, *Thoughts*, 111.

11. George H. Nash, *The Conservative Intellectual Movement in America Since 1945* (Wilmington, DE: ISI Books, 1998), xiii, 49.

12. Publius Decius Mus, "The Flight 93 Election," *Claremont Review of Books*, September 5, 2016, https://www.claremont.org/crb/basicpage/the-flight-93-election/.

13. Mus, "Flight 93."

14. American Association of University Professors, "1940 Statement of Principles on Academic Freedom and Tenure," https://www.aaup.org/report/1940-statement-principles-academic-freedom-and-tenure.

15. Steven Kautz, *Liberalism and Community* (Ithaca, NY: Cornell University Press, 1995), 217.

Chapter One: Holding Harvard to Its Word

1. I wrote about this incident in "Harvard Serves Ideology with Meals," *Commentary Magazine* Blog, December 16, 2015, www.commentarymagazine.com /american-society/harvard-serves-ideology-meals/.

2. Scott Jaschik, "Debate Over Lynch Memorial Hall: Is Name Racist?" *Inside-HigherEd*, December 9, 2015, www.insidehighered.com/quicktakes/2015/12/09 /debate-over-lynch-memorial-hall-name-racist.

3. Harvard Undergraduate Council Letter, December 16, 2015, drive.google.com /file/d/0By8LSX6DBUaHd1BodFV2TzB2bEU/view?pref=2&pli=1.

4. Lawrence Summers, interview with Bill Kristol, *Conversations with Bill Kristol* interview, January 28, 2016, conversationswithbillkristol.org/transcript/larry -summers-ii-transcript/.

5. George F. Will, "A Life Athwart History," *Washington Post*, February 9, 2008, http://www.washingtonpost.com/wp-dyn/content/article/2008/02/28 /AR2008022803230_2.html.

6. Allan Bloom, *Giants and Dwarfs, Essays 1960–1990* (New York: Simon & Schuster, 1990), 17.

7. Harvard Undergraduate Council Letter.

8. Locke, *Thoughts*, 140. See also my "A Hope for Higher Education in 2016," *Commentary Magazine* Blog, December 22, 2015, www.commentarymagazine.com /american-society/hope-higher-education-2016/.

9. Thomas Jefferson to John Adams, July 5, 1814.

10. Allan Bloom, *The Closing of the American Mind* (New York: Simon & Schuster, 1987), 136, 352–53.

11. Association of American Colleges and Universities, "About AAC&U," https:// www.aacu.org/about.

12. Association of American Colleges and Universities, "Making the Case for Liberal Education—and Its Economic Value: Talking Points," https://www.aacu.org /leap/presidentstrust/talkingpoints/.

13. Ian Wilhelm, "Remaking Liberal Education" (interview of Bergeron), *Chronicle of Higher Education*, November 20, 2016, www.chronicle.com/article/Video -Remaking-the-Liberal/238306/.

14. Bloom, *Closing*, 20–21.

15. Tocqueville, *Democracy*, 459.

16. Bloom, *Closing*, 64.

17. Jonathan Marks, "Who's Afraid of the Big Bad Disruption?" *InsideHigherEd*, October 5, 2012, https://www.insidehighered.com/views/2012/10/05/why-moocs -wont-replace-traditional-instruction-essay.

18. Max Chafkin, "Udacity's Sebastian Thrun, Godfather of Free Online Educa-tion, Changes Course," *Fast Company*, November 14, 2013, www.fastcompany.com /3021473/udacity-sebastian-thrun-uphill-climb. See also my "Education Revolution? Don't Believe the Hype or the Counter-Hype," *Commentary Magazine* Blog, Novem-ber 23, 2013, https://www.commentarymagazine.com/culture-civilization /education-revolution-dont-believe-the-hype-or-the-counter-hype/.

19. Cathy Davidson, *The New Education: How to Revolutionize the University to Prepare Students for a World in Flux* (New York: Basic Books, 2017), 91.

20. Bloom, *Closing*, 22.

21. Authors from elite institutions don't always neglect non-elite education— Delbanco, for example, although he focuses on "the so-called elite colleges," has "observed and participated in classes at a wide range of colleges with students at all levels" and is deeply concerned about so-called non-elite students. Andrew Del-banco, *College: What It Was, Is, and Should Be* (Princeton, NJ: Princeton University Press, 2012), 6, 172–73. Martha Nussbaum supplements her experience at Harvard, Brown, and the University of Chicago with visits to non-elite institutions. Martha Nussbaum, *Cultivating Humanity: A Classical Defense of Reform in Liberal Education* (Cambridge, MA: Harvard University Press, 1997), ix–xi. Neither author would deny that one learns more by spending a career at such places than by visiting them.

22. Bloom, *Closing*, 22.

23. Earl Shorris, "On the Uses of a Liberal Education: As a Weapon in the Hands of the Restless Poor," *Harper's Magazine*, September 1997, 53–54.

24. Shorris, "Restless Poor," 55.

25. Shorris, "Restless Poor," 57.

26. Earl Shorris, *The Art of Freedom: Teaching Humanities to the Poor* (New York: W.W. Norton, 2013), 114. My discussion of Shorris draws on my review of the *Art of Freedom*, "Culture Shock: There's a Reason Why They Call It the Humanities," *Weekly Standard*, August 12, 2013, 32.

27. W.E.B. Du Bois, *The Souls of Black Folk* (Mineola, NY: Dover, 1994), 51.

28. Shorris, *Freedom*, 240, 244. Consider, also, on Columbia University's Freedom and Citizenship program, Tamara Mann, "An Intimate Education," *InsideHigherEd*, January 9, 2015, www.insidehighered.com/views/2015/01/09/essay-teaching-great -books-low-income-high-school-students.

29. Du Bois, *Souls*, 59–60.

30. Alexis de Tocqueville, *Democracy*, 5, 463. On a related theme, see Zena Hitz, "Why Intellectual Work Matters," *Modern Age*, July 2017, 32–33. For a more aristo-

cratic Tocqueville, see Anthony Kronman, *The Assault on American Excellence* (New York: Free Press, 2019), 39–45.

31. Tocqueville, *Democracy*, 451.

32. Locke, *Of the Conduct of the Understanding*, in Locke, *Thoughts*, 171–72, 176–77.

33. Ruth W. Grant and Nathan Tarcov, "Introduction," in Locke, *Thoughts*, xii.

34. But for a thoughtful consideration of Franklin's limitations, see Lorraine Smith Pangle and Thomas L. Pangle, *The Learning of Liberty: The Educational Ideas of the American Founders* (Lawrence: University Press of Kansas, 1993), 278–84.

35. Bloom, *Closing*, 19–20.

Chapter Two: Left, Right, Wrong

1. Federalist No. 1, in *The Federalist Papers*, Alexander Hamilton, James Madison, and John Jay (New York: Bantam Books, 1982), 1–2.

2. Students for a Democratic Society, "The Port Huron Statement," in Richard Flacks and Nelson Lichtenstein, eds., *The Port Huron Statement: Sources and Legacies of the New Left's Founding Manifesto* (Philadelphia: University of Pennsylvania Press, 2015), 282–83. The historian Robert Cohen observes that the Statement's "ideas about the university" were influenced by "progressive and radical academics," like C. Wright Mills, already present there. If such a "politically engaged and radically democratic faculty" were "setting [the university's] tone," rather than "serving as dissidents," the university might be redeemed. Robert Cohen, "The New Left's Love-Hate Relationship with the University," in Flacks and Lichtenstein, eds., *Sources and Legacies*, 110–11.

3. Richard Rorty, *Achieving Our Country: Leftist Thought in Twentieth Century America* (Cambridge, MA: Harvard University Press, 1999), 82–83.

4. Jon A. Shields and Joshua M. Dunn, Sr., *Passing on the Right: Conservative Professors in the Progressive University* (New York: Oxford University Press, 2016), 83. I draw here on my review of *Passing*, "Elephants on the Quad," *Wall Street Journal*, April 3, 2016, A17.

5. E. B. Stolzenberg et al., *Undergraduate Teaching Faculty: The HERI Faculty Survey 2016–2017.* (Los Angeles: Higher Education Research Institute, UCLA, 2019), 38.

6. Neil Gross and Solon Simmons, "The Social and Political Views of American College and University Professors," in *Professors and Their Politics*, Neil Gross and Solon Simmons, eds. (Baltimore, MD: Johns Hopkins University Press, 2014), 31.

7. Mitchell Langbert, "Homogenous: The Political Affiliations of Elite Liberal Arts College Faculty," National Association of Scholars website, April 24, 2018, https://www.nas.org/articles/homogenous_political_affiliations_of_elite_liberal.

8. Neil Gross, *Why Are Professors Liberal and Why Do Conservatives Care?* (Cambridge, MA: Harvard University Press, 2013), 119. Some liberals are concerned about the disparity. See, for example, Michael S. Roth, "The Opening of the Liberal Mind," *Wall Street Journal*, May 11, 2017, C3.

9. On the Christakises, see Anemona Hartocollis, "Yale Professor and Wife, Targets of Protests, Resign as College Heads," *New York Times*, May 26, 2016, https://www.nytimes.com/2016/05/27/us/yale-professor-and-wife-targets-of-protests-resign-as-college-heads.html. Brett Weinstein's woes were the subject of two *New York Times* op-eds. See Bari Weiss, "When the Left Turns on Its Own," *New York Times*, June 1, 2017, https://www.nytimes.com/2017/06/01/opinion/when-the-left-turns-on-its-own.html, and Frank Bruni, "These Campus Inquisitions Must Stop," *New York Times*, June 3, 2017, https://www.nytimes.com/2017/06/03/opinion/sunday/bruni-campus-inquisitions-evergreen-state.html.

10. Nathan Honeycutt and Laura A. Freberg, "The Liberal and Conservative Experience Across Academic Disciplines: An Extension of Inbar and Lammers," *Social Psychological and Personality Science* 8, no. 2 (March 2017): 115–23. Also, George Yancey, *Compromising Scholarship: Religious and Political Bias in American Higher Education* (Waco, TX: Baylor University Press, 2011).

11. Francisco Salinas, "Connecting the Dots," School of Public Service News, Boise State University, August 14, 2017, https://web.archive.org/web/20180104085810/https://sps.boisestate.edu/blog/2017/08/connecting-the-dots/.

12. For Yenor's account, see "Take Our Colleges Back: A Blueprint for Rolling Back Campus Radicalism," *Weekly Standard*, January 22, 2018, https://www.weeklystandard.com/scott-yenor/take-our-colleges-back-a-blueprint-for-rolling-back-campus-radicalism. See also Bill Manny, "Try to Discuss Speech and Academic Freedom at Boise State, and Nuance Is the First Casualty," *Idaho Statesman*, November 10, 2017, https://www.idahostatesman.com/opinion/bill-manny/article183933246.html.

13. Shields and Dunn, *Passing*, 4.

14. Samuel Abrams, "The Contented Professors: How Conservative Faculty See Themselves within the Academy," 2016, draft accessible at https://www.researchgate.net/publication/312229229_The_Contented_Professors_How_Conservative_Faculty_See_Themselves_within_the_Academy. Abrams's experience at Sarah Lawrence College—including the vandalizing of his office and demands that his tenure be reconsidered—hasn't changed his general view. See Colleen Flaherty, "When Students Want to Review a Tenured Professor," *InsideHigherEd*, March 13, 2019, https://www.insidehighered.com/news/2019/03/13/students-sarah-lawrence-want-review-tenure-conservative-professor-who-criticized.

15. Frederick M. Hess, "When Conservative Scholars Fall Prey to Stockholm Syndrome," *National Review Online*, March 14, 2016, https://www.aei.org/publication/when-conservative-scholars-fall-prey-to-stockholm-syndrome/.

16. Caitlin Flanagan, "That's Not Funny! Today's College Students Can't Seem to Take a Joke," *The Atlantic*, September 2015, https://www.theatlantic.com /magazine/archive/2015/09/thats-not-funny/399335/.

17. Jacques Berlinerblau, *Campus Confidential: How College Works, or Doesn't, for Professors, Parents, and Students* (Brooklyn, NY: Melville House, 2017), 178, 182. Italics in the original.

18. Jonathan Chait, "Ta Nehisi Coates Disagrees with 'Jonathan Chait' and So Do I," *New York Magazine*, March 31, 2014, http://nymag.com/daily/intelligencer/2014/03 /coates-disagrees-with-jonathan-chait-so-do-i.html.

19. Ta Nehisi Coates, "Other People's Pathologies," *The Atlantic*, March 30, 2014, https://www.theatlantic.com/politics/archive/2014/03/other-peoples-pathologies /359841/.

20. In "The National Prospect: A Symposium," *Commentary Magazine*, November 1995, https://www.commentarymagazine.com/articles/the-national-prospect/.

21. Michel Foucault, "Truth and Power" (interview), in Colin Gordon, ed., *Power/Knowledge: Selected Interviews and Other Writings 1972–1977* (New York: Pantheon Books, 1980), 133.

22. Thomas Haskell, "Justifying the Rights of Academic Freedom," in *The Future of Academic Freedom*, Louis Menand, ed. (Chicago: University of Chicago Press, 1996), 83.

23. For the general argument, see especially Nussbaum, *Cultivating*, 50–84.

24. Du Bois, *Souls*, 66.

25. Bloom, *Closing*, 35.

26. Peggy McIntosh, "Unpacking the Invisible Knapsack," *Peace and Freedom Magazine*, July / August 1989, 10–12.

27. Du Bois, *Souls*, 66–67.

28. Julie Crawford, "What Columbia's Syllabus Change Says About the Evolution of Diversity," *The Observer*, December 3, 2015, http://observer.com/2015/12/what -columbias-syllabus-change-says-about-the-evolution-of-diversity/.

29. Sarah Bond, "Why We Need to Start Seeing the Classical World in Color," *Hyperallergic*, June 7, 2017, https://hyperallergic.com/383776/why-we-need-to-start -seeing-the-classical-world-in-color/.

30. Colleen Flaherty, "Threats for What She Didn't Say," *InsideHigherEd*, June 19, 2017, https://www.insidehighered.com/news/2017/06/19/classicist-finds-herself -target-online-threats-after-article-ancient-statues.

31. I draw here from my post, "Microaggressing Against Science," *Commentary Magazine* Blog, February 22, 2017, https://www.commentarymagazine.com/politics -ideas/microaggressing-against-science/.

32. Stephanie Saul, "Campuses Cautiously Train Students against Subtle Insults," *New York Times*, September 6, 2016, https://www.nytimes.com/2016/09/07/us

/campuses-cautiously-train-freshmen-against-subtle-insults.html; Tyler Kingkade, "Universities Are Trying to Teach Faculty to Spot Microaggressions," *Huffington Post*, July 19, 2015 (updated February 2, 2017), https://www.huffingtonpost.com/entry /universities-microaggressions_us_559ec77be4b096729155bfec.

33. Jeffrey Aaron Snyder and Amna Khalid, "The Rise of Bias Response Teams on Campus, *New Republic*, March 30, 2016, https://newrepublic.com/article/132195 /rise-bias-response-teams-campus.

34. Peter Schmidt, "Campaigns Against Microaggressions Prompt Big Concerns About Free Speech," *Chronicle of Higher Education*, July 9, 2015, http://www.chronicle .com/article/Campaigns-Against/231459/.

35. Scott O. Lilienfeld, "Microaggressions: Strong Claims, Inadequate Evidence," *Perspectives on Psychological Science* 12, no. 1 (2017): 143–44.

36. For one attempt to fill the gap, see Jonathan W. Kanter et al., "A Preliminary Report on the Relationship between Microaggressions Against Black People and Racism Among White College Students," *Race and Social Problems* 9, no. 4 (December 2017): 291–99.

37. Lilienfeld, "Microaggressions," 159.

38. Greg Lukianoff and Jonathan Haidt, "The Coddling of the American Mind," *The Atlantic*, September 2015, https://www.theatlantic.com/magazine/archive/2015 /09/the-coddling-of-the-american-mind/399356/. For a recent discussion of the state of microaggression research, see Monnica T. Williams, "Microaggressions: Clarification, Evidence, and Impact," *Perspectives on Psychological Science* 15, no. 1 (January 2020): 3–26, and Scott O. Lilienfeld, "Microaggression Research and Application: Clarifications, Corrections, and Common Ground," *Perspectives on Psychological Science* 15, no. 1 (January 2020): 27–37.

39. Derald Wing Sue, "Microaggressions and Evidence': Empirical or Experiential Reality," *Perspectives on Psychological Science* 12, no. 1 (2017): 171. Sue's emphasis.

40. Rorty, *Achieving*, 94.

41. Rorty, *Achieving*, 95. Andrew Sullivan, "Is Intersectionality a Religion," *New York Magazine*, March 10, 2017, http://nymag.com/daily/intelligencer/2017/03 /is-intersectionality-a-religion.html. See also William Deresiewicz, "On Political Correctness: Power, Class, and the New Campus Religion," *American Scholar*, Spring 2017, https://theamericanscholar.org/on-political-correctness/# .WXDU5oTyvIU.

42. Richard Landes provides the text of the letters at his blog, *The Augean Stables*, http://www.theaugeanstables.com/pessin-archive-introduction-and-linked -chronology/community-statements-in-chronological-order-march-24-april-26/. For more on the case, see Richard Landes, ed., *Salem on the Thames: Moral Panic, Anti-Zionism, and the Triumph of Hate Speech at Connecticut College* (Boston: Academic Studies Press, 2020).

43. Announcement of the forum can be found, thanks to Landes, at http://www
.theaugeanstables.com/pessin-archive-introduction-and-linked-chronology
/bergerons-announcement-of-all-campus-forum-march-20/. One student's account
of the forum can be found at http://www.theaugeanstables.com/pessin-archive
-introduction-and-linked-chronology/student-a-description-of-open-forum-email
-to-pessin-march-25/.

44. Bergeron's letter can be found at https://www.conncoll.edu/media/new
-media/president-bergeron/letters/March-29-2015.pdf.

45. Tina Detelj, "One Person Behind Racist Incidents at Connecticut College,"
WTNH News, April 1, 2015, https://www.wtnh.com/news/one-person-behind
-racist-incidents-at-connecticut-college/.

46. Peter Holley and Lindsey Bever, "A Racist Note Sparked Protests at a Minnesota College. The School Now Says the Message Was Fake," *Washington Post*,
May 10, 2017, https://www.washingtonpost.com/news/grade-point/wp/2017/05
/01/protests-erupt-classes-canceled-after-racist-notes-enrage-a-minnesota
-college/.

47. Here I draw on three pieces I wrote for other occasions. "Conservatives and
the 'Higher Ed. Bubble,'" *InsideHigherEd*, November 15, 2012, https://www
.insidehighered.com/views/2012/11/15/conservative-focus-higher-ed-bubble
-undermines-liberal-education-essay; "The Learning Curve," *Weekly Standard*,
March 3, 2014, http://www.weeklystandard.com/the-learning-curve/article/782741;
and "The Wrong Way to Argue About Higher Ed.," *Minding the Campus*, January 10,
2014, http://www.mindingthecampus.org/2014/01/the_wrong_way_to_argue
_about_h/.

48. Glenn Reynolds, *The Higher Education Bubble* (New York: Encounter Books,
2012).

49. Ron Lieber, "Placing the Blame as Students Are Buried in Debt," *New York
Times*, May 28, 2010, http://www.nytimes.com/2010/05/29/your-money/student
-loans/29money.html.

50. Meta Brown et al., "Grading Student Loans," *Liberty Street Economics*, March 5,
2012, https://libertystreeteconomics.newyorkfed.org/2012/03/grading-student
-loans.html.

51. *Digest of Higher Education Statistics 2016*, National Center for Education Statistics, https://nces.ed.gov/programs/digest/d16/tables/dt16_318.30.asp.

52. Susan Dynarski, a University of Michigan economist, reportedly summed up
a presentation on student loan debt this way: "If I see anyone in this room put a
women's studies major with $100,000 of debt in their article I'm going to come find
you." Kim Clark and Adam Tamburin, "Debunking the Myths Behind Student Loan
Debt," Education Writer's Association Blog, June 14, 2018, https://www.ewa.org
/blog-higher-ed-beat/debunking-myths-behind-student-loan-debt.

53. Reynolds, *Bubble*, 7, 25–26.

54. Stephanie Riegg Cellini and Rajeev Darolia, "Different Degrees of Debt: Student Borrowing in the For-Profit, Nonprofit, and Public Sectors," *Brown Center for Education at Brookings*, June 2016, 3, no. 6, 4.

55. "The Condition of Education at a Glance," National Center for Education Statistics, last updated May 2018, https://nces.ed.gov/programs/coe/indicator_cha.asp.

56. Doug Lederman, "The Incredible Shrinking Higher Ed Industry," *InsideHigherEd*, October 14, 2019, https://www.insidehighered.com/news/2019/10/14/higher-ed-shrinks-number-colleges-falls-lowest-point-two-decades.

57. Scott Jaschik, "Are Prospective Students About to Disappear?" *InsideHigherEd*, January 8, 2018, https://www.insidehighered.com/admissions/article/2018/01/08/new-book-argues-most-colleges-are-about-face-significant-decline. Rick Seltzer, "Outbreak Hurts Higher Ed Worldwide for Next Year, Moody's Says," *InsideHigherEd*, April 7, 2020.

58. Citations in this paragraph and the next are, unless otherwise noted, from Victor Davis Hanson, "The Humanities Move Off Campus," *City Journal*, Autumn 2008, https://www.city-journal.org/html/humanities-move-campus-13129.html.

59. Victor Davis Hanson, "The Outlaw Campus," *National Review Online*, January 7, 2014, http://www.nationalreview.com/article/367689/outlaw-campus-victor-davis-hanson.

60. Mus, "Flight 93."

61. William F. Buckley, *God and Man at Yale: The Superstitions of Academic Freedom* (Chicago: Regnery, 1951), xii.

62. Salvatori Center home page, https://www.cmc.edu/salvatori, last accessed July 25, 2017.

63. Toni Airaksinen, "'Manspreading' a Sign of 'Sexist Environment,' Student Claims," *Campus Reform*, July 21, 2017, https://www.campusreform.org/?ID=9468.

Chapter Three: The Importance of Being Reasonable

1. I follow Lee Ward's democratic interpretation of Locke's *Thoughts*. *Thoughts* focuses on "the sons of the politically vital gentry," but Locke "emphasizes the far-reaching implications of his educational proposals for girls" and "potentially for all classes in the nation." Lee Ward, *John Locke and Modern Life* (Cambridge: Cambridge University Press, 2010), 173.

2. Daniel Kahneman, *Thinking Fast and Slow* (New York: Farrar, Straus and Giroux, 2011).

3. Charles S. Taber and Milton Lodge, "Motivated Skepticism in the Evaluation of Political Beliefs," *American Journal of Political Science* 50, no. 3 (July 2006): 763–64.

4. Taber and Lodge, "Motivated Skepticism," 755–56.

5. Reported in Kahneman, *Thinking*, 218–20.

6. Locke, *Conduct*, 184.

7. Tocqueville, *Democracy*, 408.

8. Tocqueville, *Democracy*, 410.

9. Tocqueville, *Democracy*, 408.

10. Bloom, *Closing*, 246, 252.

11. Locke, *Conduct*, 169–71.

12. Locke, *Conduct*, 173.

13. Locke, *Thoughts*, 36.

14. Mark Edmundson, "On the Uses of a Liberal Education: As Lite Entertainment for Bored College Students," *Harper's Magazine*, September 1997, 40.

15. Edmundson, "Lite Entertainment," 41–42.

16. Greg Lukianoff and Jonathan Haidt, *The Coddling of the American Mind: How Good Intentions and Bad Ideas Are Setting Up a Generation for Failure* (New York: Penguin Press, 2018), 71.

17. Erika Christakis, "Email to Silliman College Students," October 20, 2015, https://www.thefire.org/email-from-erika-christakis-dressing-yourselves-email-to -silliman-college-yale-students-on-halloween-costumes/.

18. See Conor Friedersdorf, "The New Intolerance of Student Activism," *The Atlantic*, November 19, 2015, https://www.theatlantic.com/politics/archive/2015/11 /the-new-intolerance-of-student-activism-at-yale/414810/.

19. But, again, let's not exaggerate the influence of the campus left. Nicholas Christakis is not now languishing in social justice prison. He has been promoted to Sterling Professor, the "highest honor bestowed on Yale faculty." "Dr. Nicholas A. Christakis Named Sterling Professor of Social and Natural Science," *Yale News*, July 23, 2018, https://news.yale.edu/2018/07/23/dr-nicholas-christakis-named -sterling-professor.

20. For an extended argument that the only serious activism is evidence-based activism, see Alice Dreger, *Galileo's Middle Finger: Heretics, Activists, and One Scholar's Search for Justice* (New York: Penguin Press, 2016).

21. Locke, *Thoughts*, 86, 88.

22. Locke, *Thoughts*, 86.

23. Locke, *Thoughts*, 85.

24. Locke, *Thoughts*, 86–87.

25. James Tully, "Governing Conduct: Locke on the Reform of Thought and Behavior," in his *An Approach to Political Philosophy: Locke in Contexts* (Cambridge: Cambridge University Press, 1993), 225. For more on this objection to Locke and a detailed response, see Marks, "Principle and Practice," on which I draw here.

26. Ruth Grant, "John Locke on Custom's Power and Reason's Authority," *Review of Politics* 74, no. 4 (Fall 2012): 621.

27. Grant, "Locke," 628–29.

28. Locke, *Conduct*, 218–19.

29. John Dewey, *Individualism: Old and New* (Amherst, NY: Prometheus Books, 1999), 75.

30. Delbanco, *College*, 71–72.

31. John Dewey, *Democracy and Education: An Introduction to the Philosophy of Education* (New York: Macmillan, 1922), 370.

32. John Dewey, "The Liberal College and Its Enemies," in Jo Ann Boydston, ed., *The Middle Works*, 1899–1924, Vol. 15 (Carbondale: Southern Illinois University Press, 1983), 209.

33. Robert Maynard Hutchins, *The Higher Learning in America* (New Haven, CT: Yale University Press, 1936), 32, 71, 119.

34. Hutchins, *Higher Learning*, 87.

35. Locke, *Thoughts*, 70.

36. Locke, *Thoughts*, 69.

37. Locke, *Thoughts*, 71.

38. Locke, *Conduct*, 171.

39. Locke, *Conduct*, 167.

40. Benjamin Franklin, *Autobiography* (Mineola, NY: Dover, 1996), 45, 81.

41. Franklin, *Autobiography*, 21, 28, 61.

42. Compare Hitz, "Intellectual Work," 34–35.

43. Stanley Fish, "Stop Trying to Sell the Humanities," *Chronicle of Higher Education*, June 17, 2018, https://www.chronicle.com/article/Stop-Trying-to-Sell-the/243643.

44. Michael Oakeshott, "The Idea of a University," in Oakeshott, *The Voice of Liberal Learning*, ed. Timothy Fuller (New Haven, CT: Yale University Press, 1989), 100.

45. Plato, *Apology*, in *Four Texts on Socrates*, trans. Thomas G. West and Grace Starry West (Ithaca, NY: Cornell University Press, 1984), 81–83.

46. Shorris, "Restless Poor," 53, 56, 58.

47. Joe Ben Hoyle, *Tips and Thoughts on Improving the Teaching Process in College—A Personal Diary*, self-published, 12, https://facultystaff.richmond.edu/~jhoyle/documents/book-teaching-x.doc.pdf.

48. Locke, *Conduct*, 199–201.

49. Locke, *Conduct*, 200.

50. Locke, *Conduct*, 169.

51. Bloom, *Closing*, 21.

52. Locke, *Conduct*, 196–97.

53. Locke, *Conduct*, 210; Galileo Galilee, "The Assayer," in *Discoveries and Opinions of Galileo*, trans. and ed. Stillman Drake (New York: Doubleday, 1957), 270.

54. Bloom, *Closing*, 42.

55. Jean-Jacques Rousseau, *Emile or On Education*, trans. Allan Bloom (New York: Basic Books, 1979), 255. For justification of my reading of Rousseau, see my "Rousseau's Critique of Locke's Education for Liberty," *Journal of Politics* 74, no. 3 (July 2012): 694–706, and "Rousseau's Challenge to Locke (and to Us)," in Eve Grace and Christopher Kelly, eds., *The Challenge of Rousseau* (Cambridge: Cambridge University Press, 2013), 253–70.

56. Rousseau, *Emile*, 344.

57. Ruth Grant, "Political Theory, Political Science, and Politics," *Political Theory* 30, no. 4 (August 2002): 591.

58. Grant, "Political Theory," 587.

59. Grant, "Political Theory," 591.

60. Grant, "Political Theory," 585.

61. See Grant, "Political Theory, 583.

62. Grant, "Political Theory," 582.

63. Grant, "Political Theory," 582. Ronald Beiner calls judgment "a form of mental activity that is not bound to rules, is not subject to explicit specification of its mode of operation (unlike methodological rationality), and comes into play beyond the confines of rule-governed intelligence." Yet it "is not without rule or reason, but rather, must strive for general validity." If judgment does not exist, there is no way to break "the twin stranglehold of methodical rules and arbitrary subjectivism." Ronald Beiner, *Political Judgment* (Chicago: University of Chicago Press, 1983), 2.

64. Grant, "Political Theory," 581.

65. Grant, "Political Theory," 585.

66. Grant, "Political Theory,"582.

67. Bloom, *Closing*, 25.

68. Bacon, *Novum Organum*, trans. and ed. Peter Urbach and John Gibson (Chicago: Open Court, 1994,) 51.

69. Bacon, *Novum*, 40.

70. King, "The Power of Nonviolence," June 4, 1957, http://teachingamericanhistory.org/library/document/the-power-of-non-violence/.

71. Grant, "Political Theory," 585.

72. Grant, "Political Theory," 585.

73. Gerald Graff, *Clueless in Academe: How Schooling Obscures the Life of the Mind* (New Haven, CT: Yale University Press, 2003), 217–22.

74. It's Jordan, however.

75. Buckley, *God and Man*, 160.

76. Graff, *Clueless*, 178.

77. David Hayes, "When BS Is a Virtue," *Chronicle of Higher Education*, September 8, 2014, https://www.chronicle.com/blogs/conversation/2014/09/08/when-bs-is-a-virtue/.

78. I write about the tension between shaping reasonable people and shaping citizens in "Socrates at the Center," *InsideHigherEd*, April 18, 2013, https://www.insidehighered.com/views/2013/04/18/liberal-education-and-civic-education-need-not-go-together-essay.

79. Dana Villa, *Socratic Citizenship* (Princeton, NJ: Princeton University Press, 2001), 2. Villa thinks that dissolving "the hubristic claim to moral expertise" has moral and democratic uses and can itself be a basis for citizenship. I can't get into his interesting argument, which takes us through six different thinkers, here.

80. Thomas Hobbes, *Leviathan*, ed. J.C.A. Gaskin (Oxford: Oxford University Press, 1996), 225.

81. See, for example, James Axtell, *Wisdom's Workshop: The Rise of the Modern University* (Princeton, NJ: Princeton University Press, 2016), 45–51.

82. That's not to say that the order isn't disingenuous and worrying, as I argue in "Thank Goodness Trump Is Here to Save Free Speech on Campus," *Chronicle of Higher Education*, March 6, 2019, https://www.chronicle.com/article/Thank-Goodness-Trump-Is-Here/245828.

83. American Council of Trustees and Alumni, *What Will They Learn? A Survey of Core Requirements at Our Nation's Colleges and Universities*, 2018, 8, https://www.goacta.org/images/download/what-will-they-learn-2018-19.pdf.

84. Elizabeth A. Bennion and Melissa R. Michelson, "How to Get More College Students to Vote," *Monkey Cage* Blog, *Washington Post*, September 18, 2018, https://www.washingtonpost.com/news/monkey-cage/wp/2018/09/18/how-to-get-more-young-people-to-vote/?utm_term=.b173c893c3d8; and "How to Get College Students to Vote," *Chronicle of Higher Education*, October 17, 2018, https://www.chronicle.com/article/College-Leaders-It-s-Your/244820.

85. Martha Nussbaum, *Not for Profit: Why Democracy Needs the Humanities* (Princeton, NJ: Princeton University Press, 2010), 143.

86. Shorris, "Restless Poor," 59.

87. Martin Diamond, "On the Study of Politics in a Liberal Education," in William A. Schambra, ed., *As Far as Republican Principles Will Admit: Essays by Martin Diamond* (Washington, DC: AEI Press, 1992), 276–77.

88. Diamond, "On the Study," 278.

89. Diamond, "On the Study," 280.

90. Locke, *Thoughts*, 139, and *Conduct*, 223. See also Ward, *John Locke*, 195.

91. Christina Caron, "Barack Obama's Favorite Book of 2018 Was 'Becoming.' Here's What Else He Liked," *New York Times*, December 28, 2018, https://www.nytimes.com/2018/12/28/arts/obama-favorites-2018.html.

92. Patrick Deneen, *Why Liberalism Failed* (New Haven, CT: Yale University Press, 2018), 18.

93. Sandra Y. L. Korn, "The Doctrine of Academic Freedom," *Harvard Crimson*, February 18, 2014, https://www.thecrimson.com/column/the-red-line/article/2014 /2/18/academic-freedom-justice/.

94. American Association of University Professors, *1915 Declaration of Principles on Academic Freedom and Academic Tenure*, https://www.aaup.org/NR/rdonlyres /A6520A9D-0A9A-47B3-B550-C006B5B224E7/0/1915Declaration.pdf). This is not the place to discuss my doubts about the AAUP idea of academic freedom, but see my "Scholars and Politics," *Weekly Standard*, November 9, 2015, https://www .weeklystandard.com/jonathan-marks/scholars-and-politics.

95. Korn, "Academic Freedom."

96. Patrick Deneen, "What's Wrong with Academic Freedom?" *American Conservative*, March 5, 2014, https://www.theamericanconservative.com/2014/03/05 /academicfreedom/. All Deneen quotations in this section are from this article, unless otherwise noted.

97. Patrick Deneen, "Learning to Be Free: The Connection Between Liberal and Civic Education," in Bradley C. Watson, ed., *Western Civilization and the Academy* (Lanham, MD: Rowman & Littlefield, 2015), 74.

98. Deneen, *Liberalism*, 49

99. American Association of University Professors, *1915 Declaration*.

100. Locke, *Thoughts*, 171.

101. Grant, "Political Theory," 585.

102. Patrick Deneen, "What Is an American Conservative?" *American Conservative*, October 9, 2013, https://www.theamericanconservative.com/2013/10/09/what -is-an-american-conservative/comment-page-1/.

103. Deneen, *Liberalism*, 1.

104. Herbert J. Storing, *What the Anti-Federalists Were For* (Chicago: University of Chicago Press, 1981), 7–8, 15.

105. http://explorer.opensyllabusproject.org/. As of May 2019.

106. *The Republic of Plato*, trans. Allan Bloom (New York: Basic Books, 1968), 31.

Chapter Four: Shaping Reasonable Students

1. Donald Lazere, *Why Higher Education Should Have a Leftist Bias* (New York: Palgrave Macmillan, 2013), 27. I draw here on my review, "The Closing of the Scholarly Mind," *American Conservative*, September 26, 2014.

2. E. B. Stolzenberg et al., *The American Freshman: National Norms Fall 2017* (Los Angeles: Higher Education Research Institute, UCLA, 2019), 54.

3. Lazere, *Why Higher Education*, xvi.

4. Lazere, *Why Higher Education*, xvi–xvii.

5. Lazere, *Why Higher Education*, 76.

6. Lazere, *Why Higher Education*, 23, 26.

7. Lazere, *Why Higher Education*, 94.

8. Kevin Eagan et al., *The American Freshman: National Norms Fall 2015* (Los Angeles: Higher Education Research Institute, UCLA, 2016), 54.

9. Stolzenberg et al., *American Freshman*, 35.

10. Jean Twenge, *iGEN: Why Today's Super-Connected Kids Are Growing Up Less Rebellious, More Tolerant, Less Happy—and Completely Unprepared for Adulthood* (New York: Simon & Schuster, 2017), 269–78.

11. Marc Singer, "Teaching the MTV Learner," *Chronicle of Higher Education*, February 13, 2002, https://www.chronicle.com/article/Teaching-the-MTV-Learner/46241.

12. Sophia Sanchez, "The Millennial Learners," *InsideHigherEd*, May 10, 2016, https://www.insidehighered.com/blogs/university-venus/millennial-learners.

13. Twenge, *iGEN*, 307.

14. Twenge, *iGEN*, 308.

15. Kevin Eagan et al., *The American Freshman: Fifty Year Trends, 1996–2015* (Los Angeles: Higher Education Research Institute, UCLA, 2015), 63–64.

16. Edmundson, "Lite Entertainment," 39–40, 59.

17. Theresa MacPhail, "Are You Assigning Too Much Reading? Or Just Too Much Boring Reading?" *Chronicle of Higher Education*, January 27, 2019, https://www.chronicle.com/article/Are-You-Assigning-Too-Much/245531.

18. Jean Twenge, *Generation Me (Revised and Updated): Why Today's Young Americans Are More Confident, Assertive, Entitled—and More Miserable Than Ever Before* (New York: Simon & Schuster, 2014), 6, 21–24.

19. Jean-Jacques Rousseau, *Discourse on the Sciences and Arts*, in Roger D. Masters and Christopher Kelly, eds., *Discourse on the Sciences and Arts (First Discourse) and Polemics*, trans. Judith R. Bush et al. (Hanover, NH: University Press of New England, 1992), 5, 14.

20. Jean-Jacques Rousseau, *Discourse on the Origins of Inequality*, in Roger D. Masters and Christopher Kelly, eds., *Discourse on the Origins of Inequality (Second Discourse), Polemics, and Political Economy*, trans. Judith R. Bush et al. (Hanover, NH: University Press of New England, 1992), 66.

21. Twenge, *Me*, 105.

22. Twenge, *Me*, 24.

23. Twenge, *iGen*, 2; *Me*, 21–106.

24. Robert N. Bellah et al., *Habits of the Heart: Individualism and Commitment in American Life* (Berkeley: University of California Press, 1985).

25. Robert D. Putnam, *Bowling Alone: The Collapse and Revival of American Community* (New York: Simon & Schuster, 2000).

26. Tocqueville, *Democracy*, 403, 482.

27. Twenge, *Me*, 7.

28. Twenge, *Me*, 183, 193–94.

29. Tocqueville, *Democracy*, 409, 470.

30. Bloom, *Closing*, 25.

31. Twenge, *iGen*, 93–142. The journalist, Jesse Singal, has, however, argued that the evidence for a recent increase in anxiety among college students—as opposed to a long-term increase going back to the 1930s—is equivocal. Jesse Singal, "The Myth of the Ever-More-Fragile College Student," *The Cut*, November 13, 2015, https://www.thecut.com/2015/11/myth-of-the-fragile-college-student.html.

32. Locke, *Conduct*, 176.

33. Locke, *Conduct*, 190.

34. Locke, *Conduct*, 176.

35. Arthur Levine and Diane R. Dean, *Generation on a Tightrope: A Portrait of Today's College Student* (San Francisco: Jossey-Bass, 2012), 101, 117, 119, 121, 123.

36. Levine and Dean, *Tightrope*, 1.

37. Leah Libresco, "Here Are the Demands from Students Protesting Racism at 51 Colleges," *FiveThirtyEight*, December 3, 2015, https://fivethirtyeight.com/features/here-are-the-demands-from-students-protesting-racism-at-51-colleges/.

38. Lukianoff and Haidt, *Coddling*, 5–6, 24, 97–98, 104–5.

39. Lukianoff and Haidt, *Coddling*, 81–98.

40. Twenge, *iGen*, 3, 154. Quoted in Lukianoff and Haidt, *Coddling*, 31.

41. Twenge, *iGen*, 144.

42. Lukianoff and Haidt, *Coddling*, 171.

43. Twenge, *iGen*, 163.

44. See my review, "Bad Therapy," *Commentary Magazine* (August 2018), 63, https://www.commentarymagazine.com/articles/bad-therapy/.

45. Jonathan Rauch, *Kindly Inquisitors: The New Attacks on Free Thought* (Chicago: University of Chicago Press, 1993), 130–31; 148.

46. Twenge, *iGen*, 153.

47. Katherine Keyes et al., "National Multi-Cohort Time Trends in Adolescent Risk Preference and the Relation with Substance Use and Problem Behavior from 1976 to 2011," *Drug and Alcohol Dependence* v. 155 (2015): 267.

48. David M. Gross and Sophfronia Scott, "Living: Proceeding with Caution," *Time*, July 16, 1990, http://content.time.com/time/magazine/article/0,9171,155010,00.html.

49. I switch to the twelfth grade because the Monitoring the Future Data on eighth and tenth graders goes back only to 1991.

50. Data from Jerald G. Bachman et al., *Monitoring the Future: A Continuing Study of the Lifestyles and Values of Youth 1982*, Ann Arbor, MI: Inter-University Consortium

for Political and Social Research, https://www.icpsr.umich.edu/icpsrweb /NAHDAP/studies/09045, and Richard A. Meich et al., *Monitoring the Future: A Continuing Study of the Lifestyles and Values of Youth (12th Grade Survey)*, 2017, Ann Arbor, MI: Inter-university Consortium for Political and Social Research, https://www.icpsr.umich.edu/icpsrweb/NAHDAP/studies/37182.

51. The recession is a possible culprit. For why Lukianoff and Haidt ruled out that suspect, see *Coddling*, 152.

52. Lukianoff and Haidt, *Coddling*, 31.

53. Levine and Dean, *Tightrope*, 43–44, 47, 81.

54. Heather Mac Donald, "Get Up, Stand Up," *City Journal*, April 9, 2017, https://www.city-journal.org/html/get-up-stand-up-15109.html.

55. Foundation for Individual Rights in Education, Disinvitation Database, https://www.thefire.org/resources/disinvitation-database/. Accessed June 5, 2019. Surprisingly, attempts were down sharply in 2018. But they were back to near-record levels in 2019.

56. Kevin Eagan et al., *Fifty Year Trends*, 86–88.

57. FIRE, Student Attitudes Association Survey 2018, https://d28htnjz2elwuj .cloudfront.net/wp-content/uploads/2018/11/14114343/Tabs-Overall.pdf.

58. Knight / Newseum, "Free Expression on Campus: A Survey of U.S. College Students and U.S. Adults," 2016, https://www.knightfoundation.org/media/uploads /publication_pdfs/FreeSpeech_campus.pdf. FIRE found dramatically different results in 2018. But the wording of their question showed the cost of free speech— that "hurtful or offensive speech" would be allowed—without showing the costs of an inclusive environment, that speech would be restricted. This skewed wording may have skewed the result.

59. John Stuart Mill, *On Liberty*, ed. Elizabeth Rappaport (Indianapolis, IN: Hackett, 1978), 18–19, 44.

60. Mill, *On Liberty*, 19.

61. Mill, *On Liberty*, 46.

62. Mill, *On Liberty*, 49.

63. This section draws on my "Speech Is an Acquired Taste," *Academe Blog*, September 22, 2017, https://academeblog.org/2017/09/22/speech-is-an-acquired-taste/.

64. Mill, *On Liberty*, 33.

Chapter Five: The Boycott, Divestment, and Sanctions Movement

1. Justin Pilgreen, "SGA Approves BDS Resolution By a Two-Vote Margin," *NYULocal* Blog, December 7, 2018, https://nyulocal.com/sga-approves-bds -resolution-with-two-vote-margin-f60ffe7653ef. The resolution, later revised for

consideration by the University Senate, is available at https://docs.google.com /document/d/14JPoL5cYOkvMe84sLtEnDmcgaNsemRYmzxERxS-g-BY/edit.

2. For a mainstream treatment of the incident, see Paul Goldman and F. Brinley Bruton, "Eitam Henkin, Killed with His Wife in West Bank Shooting, Was American," *NBC News*, October 6, 2015, https://www.nbcnews.com/news/world/eitam -henkin-killed-wife-west-bank-shooting-was-american-n439161. Abunimah's tweet is at https://twitter.com/aliabunimah/status/649679336933588992.

3. Ali Abunimah, "Israel Uses Caterpillar Equipment in Apparent Extrajudicial Killing," *Electronic Intifada*, July 28, 2016. https://electronicintifada.net/blogs/ali -abunimah/israel-uses-caterpillar-equipment-apparent-extrajudicial-killing.

4. Gili Cohen, "Palestinian Who Murdered Rabbi Michael Mark Killed in West Bank Clashes, Shin Bet Confirms," *Haaretz*, July 27, 2016, https://www.haaretz.com /israel-news/palestinian-who-murdered-michael-mark-killed-shin-bet-says-1 .5416503.

5. I wrote about the NYU incident in "Professors of Shamelessness," *Commentary Magazine* Blog, November 2, 2018, https://www.commentarymagazine.com/anti -semitism/bds-professors-of-shamelessness/.

6. For more detail, see Cary Nelson's superb *Israel Denial: Anti-Zionism, Anti-Semitism, and the Faculty Campaign Against the Jewish State* (Washington, DC: Academic Engagement Network; Bloomington: Indiana University Press, 2019).

7. NGO Forum Declaration, September 3, 2001, http://www.i-p-o.org/racism -ngo-decl.htm. For one witness's story of the run-up and aftermath of the Forum, see Tom Lantos, "The Durban Debacle," *Fletcher Forum of World Affairs* 26, no. 2 (Winter/Spring 2002): 1–22.

8. "Students and Faculty at Harvard, MIT Reject Call for Israel Divestment," *Jewish Telegraphic Agency*, May 21, 2002, https://www.jta.org/2002/05/21/archive /students-and-faculty-at-harvard-mit-reject-call-for-israel-divestment.

9. Matthew Purdy, "Our Towns; On Issue of Israel, Campuses Can't Tell Left from Right," *New York Times*, November 17, 2002, https://www.nytimes.com/2002 /11/17/nyregion/our-towns-on-issue-of-israel-campuses-can-t-tell-left-from-right .html.

10. "Palestinian Civil Society Call for BDS," https://bdsmovement.net/call.

11. Sunaina Maira, *Boycott! The Academy and Justice in Palestine* (Oakland: University of California Press, 2018), 17.

12. Palestinian Boycott, Sanctions, and Divestment National Committee, "Israel's System of Apartheid Laws," July 9, 2018, https://bdsmovement.net/news/israels -system-apartheid-laws.

13. Yair Rosenberg, "NY Times, MSNBC Whitewash BDS," *Tablet*, February 6, 2013.

14. Maira, *Boycott*, 17.

15. Steven Salaita, "Normatizing State Power: Uncritical Ethical Praxis and Zionism," in Piya Chatterjee and Sunaina Maira, eds., *The Imperial University: Academic Repression and Scholarly Dissent* (Minneapolis: University of Minnesota Press, 2014), 223. Salaita, *Uncivil Rites: Palestine and the Limits of Academic Freedom* (Chicago: Haymarket Books, 2015), 17. Bruce Robbins, another university-based BDS advocate, criticizes Maira for not being even clearer than she is that BDS implies a "one state solution" (i.e., a Palestinian-majority state). Bruce Robbins, "Bruce Robbins Reviews Boycott," *Critical Inquiry Review*, September 5, 2018, https://criticalinquiry.uchicago.edu/bruce_robbins_reviews_boycott/.

16. This "academic boycott" is Maira's particular focus.

17. See my post, "At Williams College, Zionists Need Not Apply," *Commentary Magazine* Blog, May 2, 2019, https://www.commentarymagazine.com/anti-semitism/at-williams-college-zionists-need-not-apply/.

18. See my post, "Pitzer College Disgraces Itself for BDS," *Commentary Magazine* Blog, March 15, 2019, https://www.commentarymagazine.com/anti-semitism/pitzer-college-disgraces-itself-for-bds/.

19. Julie Wurth, "UI Student Government OKs Resolution Chastising Chancellor for Email on anti-Semitism," *News-Gazette*, October 25, 2019, https://www.news-gazette.com/news/local/university-illinois/ui-student-government-oks-resolution-chastising-chancellor-for-email-on/article_92f49a89-f845-513c-949b-887ed240355e.html. The resolution is available at https://jewishinsider.com/wp-content/uploads/2019/10/PDF-UIUC.pdf.

20. "Berkeley's Jewish Community Responds to 4/17 ASUC Senate Meeting," *Jewish Newspaper of California*, undated, https://www.jncberkeley.com/post/berkeley-s-jewish-community-responds-to-4-17-asuc-senate-meeting/.

21. The poster is archived at https://web.archive.org/web/20130207003849/http://www.brooklynsjp.com/.

22. Chavie Lieber, "Brooklyn College Department Signs on as Sponsor of BDS Event," *Jewish Telegraphic Agency*, January 30, 2013, https://www.jta.org/2013/01/30/united-states/brooklyn-college-department-signs-on-as-sponsor-of-bds-event; Corey Robin, "Where Does Mayor Bloomberg Stand on Academic Freedom?" Corey Robin Blog, February 4, 2013, http://coreyrobin.com/2013/02/04/where-does-mayor-bloomberg-stand-on-academic-freedom/; Greenwald's comments are available via the Gatestone Institute, at https://www.gatestoneinstitute.org/3573/letter-brooklyn-college-glenn-greenwald#questions; Judith Butler, "Judith Butler's Remarks to Brooklyn College on BDS," *The Nation*, February 17, 2013, https://www.thenation.com/article/judith-butlers-remarks-brooklyn-college-bds/. This paragraph draws on my "Department of Excuses: BDS at Brooklyn College," *Jewish Ideas Daily*, February 12, 2013, http://www.jewishideasdaily.com/5935/features/department-of-excuses-bds-at-brooklyn-college/.

23. https://twitter.com/CoreyRobin/status/297222529599279104.

24. The letter is available at https://www.scribd.com/document/123394756 /Letter-from-Lew-Fidler.

25. Kate Taylor, "Mayor Backs College's Plan to Welcome Critics of Israel," *New York Times*, February 6, 2013, https://www.nytimes.com/2013/02/07/nyregion /bloomberg-defends-brooklyn-colleges-right-to-bds-talk.html.

26. A detailed report, conducted for Brooklyn College by an outside law firm, can be found at https://cuny.edu/about/administration/chancellor/BDS_REPORT.pdf.

27. Maira, *Boycott*, 81.

28. Maira, *Boycott*, 120.

29. Sunaina Maira, "Guest Editor's Preface," *Journal of Asian American Studies* 9, no. 2 (June 2006): xii.

30. Ibrahim G. Aoude, "Arab Americans and Ethnic Studies," *Journal of Asian American Studies* 9, no. 2 (June 2006): 149.

31. Maira, "Guest Editor's Preface," xiii.

32. Maira, *Boycott*, 79, 169.

33. Karl Marx, "On the Jewish Question," in Robert C. Tucker, ed., *The Marx-Engels Reader*, Second Edition (New York: W.W. Norton, 1978), 42.

34. Karl Marx, *The Communist Manifesto*, in Tucker, ed., *Reader*, 485.

35. Maira, *Boycott*, 36, 169.

36. Maira, *Boycott*, 131.

37. Maira, *Boycott*, 119.

38. Maira, *Boycott*, 131.

39. Hannah Allam, "U.S. Denies Entry to Leader of Movement to Boycott Israel," *NPR*, April 11, 2019, https://www.npr.org/2019/04/11/712189791/u-s-denies-entry -to-leader-of-movement-to-boycott-israel.

40. Corey Robin Blog, "A Challenge to Critics of BDS," January 10, 2014, http:// coreyrobin.com/2014/01/10/a-challenge-to-critics-of-bds/.

41. Maira, *Boycott*, 169.

42. On its website, https://www.bdsmovement.net/bnc.

43. The full statement is available at https://bdsmovement.net/news/solidarity -palestinian-popular-resistance-boycott-israel-now.

44. US Campaign for the Academic and Cultural Boycott of Israel Blog, "US-ACBI Call for Solidarity with the Palestinian People: Boycott Now!" https://usacbi .org/2015/10/usacbi-call-for-solidarity-with-the-palestinian-people-boycott-now/. The post is undated but was widely shared on October 15, 2015. I've written about BDS and nonviolence in "BDS Nonviolence Provides Cover for Violent Allies," James G. Martin Center for Academic Renewal website, October 30, 2015, https:// www.jamesgmartin.center/2015/10/bds-nonviolence-provides-cover-for-violent -allies/.

45. David M. Halbfinger, Michael Wines, and Steven Erlanger, "Is B.D.S. Anti-Semitic? A Closer Look at the Israel Boycott Campaign," *New York Times*, July 27, 2019, https://www.nytimes.com/2019/07/27/world/middleeast/bds-israel-boycott-antisemitic.html.

46. Maira, *Boycott*, 57.

47. Alan Wolfe, "Anti-American Studies," in Wolfe, *An Intellectual in Public* (Ann Arbor: University of Michigan Press), 2003, 42–60. A list of associations endorsing the boycott can be found at https://usacbi.org/academic-associations-endorsing-boycott/.

48. Maira, *Boycott*, 56.

49. Maira, *Boycott*, 50.

50. Amitai Etzioni, "Harsh Lessons in Incivility," *Chronicle Review* 49, no. 10 (November 1, 2002), https://www.chronicle.com/article/Harsh-Lessons-in-Incivility/32365.

51. The "Letter Against Expulsion of the Palestinians" is available at http://web.archive.org/web/20021219141415/http://www.professorsofconscience.org/.

52. MESA maintains a list of past presidents and board members here: https://mesana.org/about/previous-boards.

53. For additional instances of anti-Israel activity on campuses long preceding the most recent boycott, see Gil Troy, *Moynihan's Moment: America's Fight Against Zionism as Racism* (Oxford: Oxford University Press, 2013), 238–39.

54. I wrote about this incident in "The Uncritical and Intemperate Partisans of the Boycott Israel Movement," *Commentary Magazine* Blog, August 8, 2014, https://www.commentarymagazine.com/foreign-policy/middle-east/israel/the-uncritical-and-intemperate-partisans-of-the-boycott-israel-movement/.

55. See Elizabeth Redden, "Breach of Duty or Legal Overreach?" *InsideHigherEd*, December 11, 2017, https://www.insidehighered.com/news/2017/12/11/lawsuit-accuses-american-studies-association-officers-concealing-their-plans-boycott.

56. Maira, *Boycott*, 126.

57. Tithi Bhattacharya and Bill V. Mullen, "Salaita's Firing Shows Where Zionism Meets Neoliberalism at US Universities," in Ashley Dawson and Bill V. Mullen, eds., *Against Apartheid: The Case for Boycotting Israeli Universities* (Chicago: Haymarket Books, 2015), 203.

58. Jewish Voice for Peace, "About Deadly Exchange," https://deadlyexchange.org/about-deadly-exchange/. I've written about this campaign in "Can the Left Recognize Anti-Semitism in Its Ranks?" *Commentary Magazine* Blog, January 14, 2019, https://www.commentarymagazine.com/anti-semitism/disgrace-at-uc-davis-anti-semitism/. While Jewish Voice for Peace has not taken responsibility for the implicit anti-Semitism of the Deadly Exchange campaign, it now concedes that injudicious comparisons of the sort it has, in fact, encouraged, help "antisemitic tropes"

thrive. "Update on the Deadly Exchange Campaign from Jewish Voice for Peace,"
https://jewishvoiceforpeace.org/update-on-deadly-exchange-campaign/.

59. "Resolution to Support the Boycott of Israel Academic Institutions," http://
aaastudies.org/wp-content/uploads/2014/12/aaas-4_20_13-conference-resolution
-to-support-the-boycott-of-israeli-academic-institutions.pdf.

60. See my "To Professors of Asian American Studies," *InsideHigherEd*, May 16,
2013, https://www.insidehighered.com/views/2013/05/16/open-letter-about-israel
-boycott-professors-asian-american-studies. For this section, I draw extensively on
that open letter and on my "How BDS Is Undermining Academic Freedom," *Mosaic*,
April 18, 2018, https://mosaicmagazine.com/observation/israel-zionism/2018/04
/how-bds-is-undermining-academic-freedom/.

61. Jonathan Marks, "To Professors."

62. However, two professors in the field signed a letter against a subsequent boycott. Russell Berman, "Opposing the Israel Boycott by the American Studies Association," *TELOSscope* Blog, December 10, 2013, http://www.telospress.com/opposing
-the-israel-boycott-by-the-american-studies-association/.

63. Berlinerblau, *Campus Confidential*, 182.

64. Shields and Dunn, *Passing*, 28.

65. I can't get into these efforts, ranging from lawsuits to legislation to federal
investigations against BDS, which are likely to get a boost from President Trump's
December 2019 Executive Order on Combating Anti-Semitism. Some of these efforts are defensible, as I explain in "A Reluctant Campus Acknowledges Zionism,"
Commentary Magazine Blog, March 22, 2019. However, I agree with professor of law
Steve Lubet that deploying the machinery of government against BDS is usually unwise
strategically, because it allows BDS advocates to portray themselves as victims, and often
unsound in principle because it carves out an exception to free speech principles that
many BDS opponents otherwise advocate. Steve Lubet, "The Wrong Way to Oppose
BDS (Again)," *Faculty Lounge* Blog, April 21, 2016, https://www.thefacultylounge.org
/2016/04/the-wrong-way-to-oppose-bds-again.html, and "The Wrong Way to Resist
Boycotts," *Faculty Lounge* Blog, December 3, 2015, https://www.thefacultylounge.org
/2015/12/the-wrong-way-to-resist-bds.html. Lubet addresses lawsuits in particular, but
his argument applies to other government-backed interventions.

66. Dean Eldredge is quoted in "Foundation for Individual Rights Letter to Fordham University," January 2017, https://www.thefire.org/fire-letter-to-fordham
-university-january-2017/. I wrote about this case in "Was Fordham Right to Ban a
Pro-Palestinian Club?" *Minding the Campus*, January 29, 2017, https://www
.mindingthecampus.org/2017/01/29/was-fordham-right-to-ban-a-pro-palestinian
-club/. For a dissenting view, see Jay Schalin, "In Defense of Excluding Antisocial
Student Groups," James G. Martin Center for Academic Renewal website, https://
www.jamesgmartin.center/2017/02/defense-excluding-antisocial-student-groups/.

67. *Healy v. James*, 408 U.S. 187 (1972).

68. The judgment is here: https://ccrjustice.org/sites/default/files/attach/2019 /07/114_8-6-19_Amended%20order.pdf.

69. *Healy v. James*, 408 U.S.180, italics and citations omitted.

70. Locke, *Conduct*, 169.

71. Hank Reichman, "Ugly Blacklist Posters Spur Resistance," *Academe Blog*, November 2, 2016, https://academeblog.org/2016/11/02/ugly-blacklist-posters-spur -resistance/.

72. The video can be found here: https://www.youtube.com/watch?v=LJgXa1Pf8po. I learned of it through David Greenberg et al., "The Blacklist in the Coal Mine," *Tablet*, October 26, 2016, https://www.tabletmag.com/scroll/216271/the-blacklist-in-the-coal -mine-canary-missions-fear-mongering-agenda-college-campuses.

73. Adriana Chaviva Freedman, "Doctor Who Tweeted About Giving Jews Wrong Meds Went to Jewish Medical School," *The Forward*, April 8, 2019, https:// forward.com/fast-forward/422199/doctor-who-tweeted-about-giving-jews-wrong -meds-went-to-jewish-medical/.

74. I've chosen not to link the profile.

75. Harry Onickel, "In Defense of Canary Mission," *Frontpage Magazine*, April 22, 2019, https://www.frontpagemag.com/fpm/273537/defense-canary-mission-harry -onickel.

76. For the endorsement, see *Hawblog*, April 27, 2014, http://blog.historians againstwar.org/2014/04/haw-info-haw-proposes-work-on.html. The resolution is here: https://www.historians.org/annual-meeting/resources-and-guides/business -meeting/resolution-to-be-considered-at-the-january-2016-business-meeting. I wrote about this incident in "Death of an anti-Israel Resolution," *Commentary Magazine* Blog, January 11, 2016, https://www.commentarymagazine.com/foreign-policy /middle-east/israel/death-anti-israel-resolution/.

77. Jeffrey Herf, "Why Historians Should Vote Down the Resolution Critical of Israel," *History News Network*, January 3, 2016, https://historynewsnetwork.org /article/161618.

78. Alliance for Academic Freedom, "Arguments against the Resolution at the Jan. 9, 2016 AHA Business Meeting," January 5, 2016, https://web.archive.org/web /20160117045148/https://thirdnarrative.org/wp-content/uploads/2016/01 /Arguments-2016-Jan-5.pdf.

79. Herf, "Why Historians." Herf's emphasis.

80. Herf, "Historians Reject Anti-Israel Resolutions," *American Interest*, January 19, 2015, https://www.the-american-interest.com/2015/01/19/historians-reject -anti-israel-resolutions/. Herf's emphasis.

81. Jeffrey Kopstein, "Loud and Fast Versus Slow and Quiet: Responses to Anti-Israel Activism on Campus," in Andrew Pessin and Doron S. Ben-Atar, eds., *Anti-Zionism*

on Campus: The University, Free Speech, and BDS (Bloomington: Indiana University Press, 2018), 142–43. I wrote about Kopstein's argument in "Fighting Anti-Zionism Slowly, Quietly, and Well," *Commentary Magazine* Blog, September 6, 2018, https://www.commentarymagazine.com/anti-semitism/fighting-anti-zionism-slowly-quietly-and-well/.

82. Kopstein, "Loud and Fast," 146.

83. Kopstein, "Loud and Fast," 143.

84. Anonymous course evaluation, Fall 2016.

Conclusion

1. Kopstein, "Loud and Fast," 143, 150.

2. Kopstein, "Loud and Fast," 146.

3. All quotations in this and the next paragraph are from Sohrab Ahmari, "Against David French-ism," *First Things*, May 29, 2019, https://www.firstthings.com/web-exclusives/2019/05/against-david-french-ism.

4. David French, "What Sohrab Ahmari Gets Wrong," *National Review Online*, May 30, 2019, https://www.nationalreview.com/2019/05/david-french-response-sohrab-ahmari/.

5. Ahmari, "Frenchism."

6. Foundation for Individual Rights in Education, "History," https://www.thefire.org/about-us/history/.

7. David French, "Against Cultural Defeatism," *National Review*, June 4, 2019, https://www.nationalreview.com/2019/06/against-conservative-cultural-defeatism/.

8. Foundation for Individual Rights in Education, "Adopting the Chicago Statement," https://www.thefire.org/get-involved/student-network/take-action/adopting-the-chicago-statement/. That "sixty-three" is as of June 5, 2019. "Chicago Statement: University and Faculty Body Support," https://www.thefire.org/c.hicago-statement-university-and-faculty-body-support/.

9. Yale University, Directed Studies, "About Us," https://directedstudies.yale.edu/about-us-0.

10. Roger Kimball, "PC Insanity May Mean the End of American Universities," *New York Post*, May 31, 2019, https://nypost.com/2019/05/31/pc-insanity-may-mean-the-end-of-american-universities/.

11. Kopstein, "Loud and Fast," 150.

12. Bloom, *Closing*, 22.

13. Heterodox Academy, "FAQ," https://heterodoxacademy.org/about-us/faqs/. Others, an earlier report explains, selected "prefer not to say," "unclassifiable," or "other." Jonathan Haidt, "Krugman Is Wrong—We Are Neither Conservative nor Outraged," Heterodox Academy Blog, February 24, 2016 (updated to include data as

of June 26, 2017), https://heterodoxacademy.org/krugman-is-wrong-we-are-neither-conservative-nor-outraged/.

14. Jonathan Haidt, "It's Finally Out: The Big Review Paper on the Lack of Political Diversity in Social Psychology," Heterodox Academy Blog, https://heterodoxacademy.org/bbs-paper-on-lack-of-political-diversity/.

15. As of June 14, 2020. Heterodox Academy, "Heterodox Academy Member Database," https://heterodoxacademy.org/about-us/members/.

16. Robert George, interview with Bill Kristol, *Conversations with Bill Kristol*, April 11, 2016, https://conversationswithbillkristol.org/transcript/robert-george-transcript/; conversation with Arthur C. Brooks, American Enterprise Institute Annual Dinner, September 26, 2016, https://www.aei.org/spotlights/annual-dinner-2016/.

17. Kassy Dillon, "College Newspaper Writer Says It's 'Fine' That Conservatives 'Feel Their Beliefs Aren't Welcome on Our Campus,'" *The Daily Wire*, February 8, 2019, https://www.dailywire.com/news/college-newspaper-says-its-ok-conservatives-dont-kassy-dillon; Rod Dreher shared the student's column on Twitter (https://twitter.com/roddreher/status/1094328336736755712?lang=en); Fox & Friends coverage from February 10 can be found here: https://news.yahoo.com/washington-university-newspaper-staff-writer-151959797.html.

18. Elizabeth Phelan, "Washington University Reflects on Free Speech with Nadine Strossen," *Student Life*, August 28, 2019, https://www.studlife.com/news/2019/08/28/washington-university-reflects-on-free-speech-with-nadine-strossen/

19. Hutchins, *Higher Learning*, 4–5.

20. Donald N. Levine, *Powers of the Mind: The Reinvention of Liberal Learning in America* (Chicago: University of Chicago Press, 2006), 5.

21. "The Students Are All Right," *Washington Examiner*, September 3, 2019, https://www.washingtonexaminer.com/opinion/op-eds/the-students-are-all-right.

22. Lukianoff and Haidt, *Coddling*, 268.

INDEX

Association for Asian American
Studies, 145, 150, 158–60
Association of American Colleges and
Universities (AAC&U), 10–11, 63
Atlanta University, 18
authority: demagogues and, 93, 154;
importance of being reasonable
and, 64–66, 75–76, 84, 86, 88, 103,
106, 111; old books and, 86; politics
and, 173
Autobiography (Franklin), 81–82

Bacon, Francis, 95–96
Bard College, 17
Barghouti, Omar, 147–48, 152
Beiner, Ronald, 194n63
Beinin, Joel, 155
Bellah, Robert, 122
Benedict XVI, 107
Bennett, William, 55
Bennion, Elizabeth A., 101
Bergeron, Katherine, 10, 53
Berlinerblau, Jacques, 37–38, 41, 160
Beyond the University (Roth), 16
bias: anti-Semitism and, 53, 146,
157–58, 163–64, 168, 171; Boycott,
Divestment, and Sanctions (BDS)
movement and, 141, 146, 157–58,
163–64, 168–69; confirmation, 114;
importance of being reasonable
and, 65, 68, 111; knowledge and, 65;
Lazere on, 115–17; politics and,
39–40, 49, 171; prejudice and, 6–7,
12–13, 15, 32–33, 42, 44, 50, 54, 64–66,
76, 87, 103, 114–16; shaping students
and, 114–17
Bloom, Allan: Buckley and, 3, 60–62,
111; *The Closing of the American Mind*
and, 3, 9, 12–13, 28, 61, 95; Deneen
and, 107–8; humanities and, 9;

importance of being reasonable
and, 67, 87, 95, 107, 111; liberalism
and, 3, 9, 12–13, 15–16; multiculturalism and, 45; politics and, 45, 60–62,
176; shaping students and, 124;
Tocqueville and, 67
Bloomberg, Michael, 148
Bond, Sarah E., 48
Book of Job, 22
Boycott, Divestment, and Sanctions
(BDS) movement: activism and,
141, 143–44, 147, 149, 152–54, 160,
167–68; argument and, 152, 161,
165–66, 169; Association for Asian
American Studies and, 145, 150,
158–60; Barghouti and, 147–48, 152;
bias and, 141, 146, 157–58, 163–64,
168–69; Brooklyn College and,
147–48, 152; Butler and, 147–48;
civil rights and, 142, 149, 154; conservatism and, 161; cultural issues and,
145, 150–51, 153; evidence and, 142,
165–69; exaggeration and, 151–58;
fear of criticizing, 43; FIRE and,
133–35, 174–76; Harvard and, 155;
importance of being reasonable
and, 146–49; Israel and, 27–28,
141–58, 161–69; Jews and, 144–46,
156–57, 163–64, 167–68; judgment
and, 147, 166–67; Kopstein and,
167–69, 171–72, 176–79; liberalism
and, 143, 149, 153, 158, 168; Locke
and, 163; Maira on, 144–45, 149–59;
Marxism and, 150–51, 160–61; moral
issues and, 158–61, 165; opposing,
160–69; partisanship and, 147;
philosophy and, 162, 169; politicization and, 42–43; politics and, 143,
148–49, 151, 153–54, 160, 168; Port
Huron Statement and, 149, 162;

politics (*continued*)
52, 172, 180; New Left and, 30; offenses and, 36–37, 49, 72, 116, 129, 134–35; partisanship and, ix, 42–44, 48, 173, 176; philosophy and, 25, 45, 52, 173; politicization and, 31, 38, 42–46, 55, 143, 160, 168; propaganda and, 45, 49, 171, 176; protests and, 46, 54, 175; racism and, 41, 49–50, 53–54; radicals and, 30, 41, 174; rationality and, 29–30, 176, 181; of refusal, 149; science and, 26, 32, 49, 51, 90, 92, 147, 177; study of, 90–91; stupidity from, 29, 64–68; surveys and, 31–33, 35, 174, 181; tradition and, 38, 41, 56, 58, 60, 173; as war and enmity, 172–76; Yale and, 33, 37, 60, 175

Popular Front for the Liberation of Palestine, 154

populism, 3

Port Huron Statement, 30, 37, 149, 162

poverty, 16, 74

"Power of Nonviolence, The" (King), 96

prejudice: bias and, 6–7, 12–13, 15, 32–33, 42, 44, 50, 54, 64–66, 76, 87, 103, 114–16; liberalism and, 6–7, 12–13, 15; Locke on, 65; shaping students and, 114–16

Princeton University, 19, 22, 174, 178

principles, 44, 67, 74, 102, 111, 154

propaganda: Boycott, Divestment, and Sanctions (BDS) movement and, 142, 149, 162–63, 168–69; importance of being reasonable and, 95; politics and, 45, 49, 171, 176; shaping students and, 116

Protestants, 49

protests: activism and, 28, 30, 33, 46, 54, 71, 96, 98, 106, 121, 127, 133, 135, 142, 146, 175; Boycott, Divestment, and Sanctions (BDS) movement and, 142, 146; importance of being reasonable and, 71, 96, 98, 106; King and, 96; liberalism and, 33; media portrayal of, 71; nonviolent, 96–97, 153–54; Palestinian issue and, 28, 142; politics and, 46, 54, 175; Port Huron Statement and, 30, 37, 149, 162; St. Olaf College and, 54; shaping students and, 121, 127, 133, 135; shutting down speeches and, 46; status quo and, 106; violence and, 48, 96–97, 128–29, 133, 136, 153–54; violent, 133; Yale and, 33, 175

psychology, 49–50, 64–65, 117

public opinion, 100, 121, 174

Purdy, Matthew, 143

Putnam, Robert, 122

racism: anti-Semitism and, 53, 146, 157–58, 163–64, 168, 171; apartheid and, 141, 143–45, 147, 153, 162, 171; bias and, 39–40; Boycott, Divestment, and Sanctions (BDS) movement and, 143–44; colonialism and, 151, 153; discrimination and, 115–17; ethnic cleansing and, 155; graffiti and, 53–54; importance of being reasonable and, 106; Israel and, 141–47, 153, 162, 171; politics and, 41, 49–50, 53–54; shaping students and, 117, 125; UN World Conference Against Racism and, 143

radicals, xiv; Boycott, Divestment, and Sanctions (BDS) movement and, 145, 149, 155, 161, 164; importance of being reasonable and, 88, 104–5,

107; liberalism and, 4; politics and,
30, 41

rationality: Boycott, Divestment, and
Sanctions (BDS) movement and,
160; importance of being reasonable and, 63, 65, 67, 69, 71, 73–74, 88,
95, 103–6, 111; liberalism and, 5–6, 24,
26; Locke on, 73–74; politics and,
29–30, 176, 181; shaping students
and, 117, 120, 127, 129, 132; usefulness
and, 12, 19, 26, 74, 80–85, 89, 103

Rauch, Jonathan, 129

reform, 28, 52, 60, 62

relativism, 60, 97, 124–25

religion, 1, 49, 69, 101, 107, 110, 123, 125,
154, 163, 174

Republicans, 32, 102, 116, 134, 136

Republic (Plato), 110–11

Reynolds, Glenn, 54–55, 57–58

Road to Serfdom, The (Hayek), 161

Robin, Corey, 147, 150, 153

Roosevelt University, 61

Rorty, Richard, 30–31, 51–52

Rosenberg, Yair, 144

Roth, Michael, 16

Rousseau, Jean-Jacques, 7, 88–89, 91,
121, 161

safety, 126–32

St. Augustine, 47

St. John's College, 20

St. Olaf College, 54

Salaita, Steven, 145, 156–57

San Francisco State University, 155

science: importance of being reasonable and, 71, 77–78, 87, 90–97, 101;
liberalism and, 10, 23, 26; natural, 71,
95; politics and, 26, 32, 49, 51, 90,
92–94, 147, 177; shaping students
and, 126; social, 32, 71, 177

self-censorship, 40

selfishness, 29, 31, 101, 121–23

settlers, 142, 144, 151, 153, 156

sex, 2, 15, 46, 73, 89, 106–7, 117, 125,
128–29

Shakespeare, 46, 70, 152

shame, ix; Boycott, Divestment, and
Sanctions (BDS) movement and,
148, 164, 172; call-out culture
and, 71–72; constructive, 68–71;
importance of being reasonable
and, 68–78, 85, 111; Locke and, 69;
Rorty and, 31; shaping students
and, 121–22

shaping students: academic freedom
and, 43, 45, 105–8, 111, 148; activism
and, 127, 133; argument and, 116,
133–38; attention span and, 118;
Bloom on, 124; citizenship and, 6,
26, 58, 99–102; civic education, 73,
82, 99–104; complex ideas and, 67;
conservatism and, 116–17, 122, 133,
136; convictions and, 36, 129; cultural
issues and, 116, 119–20, 128; education
as exorcism and, 51–54; elitism and,
115; evidence and, 114–17, 121, 126, 129,
134, 138; Foundation for Individual
Rights in Education (FIRE) and,
133–35, 174–76; free speech and,
132–39; Generation Me and, 121–23;
Generation Z and, 117–20, 122, 124,
126, 128–31, 133–34; indoctrination
and, 37–41, 75, 171, 174; Israel and,
136; judgment and, 90–99, 113–14,
121–22, 135; liberalism and, 116–17,
136; Locke and, 75, 125–26, 133, 138;
mental health and, 49–51, 125, 128;
Millennials and, 118, 131; moral
issues and, 121, 124; old books and,
85–90; opacity of students and,

CPSIA information can be obtained
at www.ICGtesting.com
Printed in the USA
JSHW030537121222
34697JS00002B/2